SPACE AND SOCIETY 2

INTERACTION

Andrew Kirby and David Lambert

LONGMAN

LONGMAN GROUP LIMITED
Longman House
Burnt Mill, Harlow, Essex CM20 2JE, England
and Associated Companies throughout the world.

First published 1984
ISBN 0 582 35353 X

Set in 10/11pt Baskerville, Linotron 202

Printed in Singapore by
The Print House (Pte) Ltd

Acknowledgements

We are grateful to the following for permission to reproduce copyright material:

BBC Publications and Angus and Robertson Publishers for extracts from *America* by Alistair Cooke; Penguin Books Ltd for extracts from *Green and Pleasant Land* by Howard Newby (Pelican Books 1980) pp. 192, 124, 124–5, copyright © Howard Newby 1979.

We are grateful to the following for permission to reproduce photographs:

Ministry of Agriculture, Fisheries and Food, page 79; Punch, page 76; Rex Features, page 78; Trinidad Guardian, page 77.

Contents

Preface

To the teacher

Aims

This series is designed for use within the sixth form as a back-up to the now familiar texts such as Tidswell's *Pattern and Process in Human Geography*, Bradford and Kent's *Human Geography* and Haggett's *Modern Synthesis*. We have designed the books as 'readers', that is, free-standing volumes that elaborate on particular topics, fleshing out the bare bones introduced within the textbook by presenting extracts from original sources and illustrative exercises. The latter are particularly important, as the emphasis throughout the series is upon the practical application of ideas, models and theories, rather than the abstract discussion of such deductive concepts. In this sense, the aim is to use the student's existing experiences of the 'real world' as a foundation for investigation, in order that these can be channelled into a systematic understanding of basic geographic principles.

Organisation

This book can be used in three ways. It is intended for use as a whole; in other words, the student should be able to use both the practical material and the original extracts in approaching a particular topic. In some instances, however, this may not be required. In such cases, it should be possible to use the practical examples alone or, if required, the published extracts as reference material.

Within each volume, a standard format is used. The authors' text is interspersed with secondary material, and at the end of each section there are questions, a check-list and notes which are designed to highlight the key issues that have been introduced. The latter are referred to throughout the text.

To the student

This book is one of a series of geography 'readers'. This means that the aim of the series is not to provide a complete source of facts and information for your sixth-form course; instead the intention is to provide a firm grounding in some of the fundamental ideas within the subject.

You should aim to read the volumes in the series as a back-up to your course. If you have problems in understanding some sections, discuss them with your teacher. There are, however, check-lists of key issues at the end of each chapter which you should refer to, and many of the ideas will become clearer as you work through the examples.

1
Movement and interaction

1.1 What determines mobility?

In the first book in this series, we considered the ways in which space is divided into many types of regions, some administrative, some natural, some functional. In this book, we want to examine the ways in which we use space, our need to travel and the constraints upon our movement. On a day-to-day basis, we all have to make certain journeys, to school, to work, to the shops, to see friends and relatives. Equally, we all face particular constraints: these journeys cannot involve too much physical effort, nor can they take up too much time or cost too much money. As a result, patterns of movement tend to be rather predictable, because people try to minimise the time and money that they spend on travel.

This principle (which has been termed the 'principle of least effort') does not of course mean that we are all able to behave in exactly the same way. MOBILITY depends upon a whole series of factors:

1. *Age* Both the very young and the old are immobile because of their physical incapacity. Medical research shows that for these groups, walking as little as 1 km can be extremely demanding. As a result, children and the aged are very dependent upon friends, neighbours and relatives when travelling.

2. *Income* Personal mobility is positively related to income – the wealthy can take an aeroplane rather than a train, and use private transport in preference to public transport.

3. *Sex* Although some families own several cars, which means that both parents, and even the children, possess individual mobility, it is usually the case that the family's breadwinner (often a man) uses the household car, thus reducing the opportunities available to the spouse remaining at home (often a woman).

4. *Location* Transport opportunities vary greatly from place to place. Some locations possess (urban) motorways, underground or rapid-transit systems (London, Newcastle, Glasgow, San Francisco, Hong Kong) and extensive bus services. Other local-

Pensions and pints at the post office pub

by JUDITH JUDD

TAKING a pint with your pension is becoming a popular pastime in the Oxfordshire village of Swalcliffe (population 250).

Last orders at the Stag's Head last week included a first-class stamp, a postal order and half-a-dozen pensions.

The village post office has just been transferred to the pub, and, though you cannot buy stamps over the pub counter—that is against Post Office regulations—the new sub-post office entrance is just outside the front door.

As the pub sign puts it: 'Stag's Head, terraced beer garden, luncheons, bar snacks, coffee, Swalcliffe post office.' And 'time' for the drinkers means 'time' for the customers at the post office which is open from 10.30 a.m. to 2.30 p.m. Monday to Saturday.

Mrs Felicia Hancock, the landlord's wife, offered to be postmistress after the village shop which served as the post office was sold and converted to a private house.

The Post Office insisted on a separate entrance so the Hancocks converted an old bottle store in a corner of their seventeenth-century pub.

Mrs Hancock says: 'I felt I had to take it on. This is a tiny village and we are very cut off. There are only a couple of buses during the day into Banbury, which is six miles away. The nearest sub-post office is in Tadmarton, the next village.

'Most pensioners don't have cars and the disappearance of the post office would have made it very difficult for them to collect their pensions.

'The Post Office has kindly let me have more or less pub hours, which means it will not be open as long as it was before. But I also help in the pub and it would have been impossible to manage more. I hope it will help keep the village alive.'

Mrs Hancock's words were echoed last week in a report on rural deprivation produced by the Association of County Councils which says that life is becoming increasingly hard for many country-dwellers.

The survey, which contains an appeal for more Government funds for country areas, says 'a whole way of life will disappear' unless more cash is forthcoming.

The influx of middle-class commuters, says the survey, has made things worse for the handicapped and elderly who have lived in villages all their lives.

'The conspicuous affluence of many of these newcomers has served both to conceal and to intensify the problems of those whose lives have closer economic and social ties with the area.'

Increasing car ownership has made life easier for some country-dwellers, but it has undermined public transport and contributed to the decline of village services.

The economic pressure which has caused the closure of many village shops has also affected many local authority services, which cost more to provide in the country than in cities.

A questionnaire from the association, answered by 42 counties, shows that 700,000 people were in parishes without a sub-post office and about 600,000 were without a food shop.

One Swalcliffe resident is particularly delighted that its sub-post office has been saved. Bill Stratford, who at 91 is the oldest inhabitant and a lifetime regular at the Stag's Head says: 'We were all very worried when we heard the shop was closing but this new arrangement is even better. I can come down and collect my pension and have a chat and a light ale at the same time.'

Figure 1.1   Example of immobility problems in rural Oxfordshire

ities however are very poorly served; rural areas in Britain are an obvious example. As fuel prices have risen, the cost of providing public transport to widely scattered communities has led to a withdrawal of services, with the result that country-dwellers are dependent upon more expensive private cars (approximately 70 per cent of households in rural areas own cars, as opposed to 56 per cent in Britain as a whole). The problems of rural dwellers are illustrated in figure 1.1.

5. *Technology* We should also bear in mind that our assumptions concerning mobility are very much based on our experience here in the United Kingdom. In developing countries, for example, personal mobility is severely restricted by the low level of transport technology. This means that, say, leisure trips are very rare, although on the other hand essential journeys (such as water collection) may involve long distances, often undertaken on foot. This is in stark contrast to the experience in the United States or Australia, where multi-lane freeways and even personal aircraft permit long journeys even for social outings.

We all need therefore to be mobile; however, some of us are more mobile than others. Let us now examine some of the factors that dictate movement patterns.

1.2 Spatial interaction

Mobility implies that people have an ability to move – the ways that they put this into practice will, however, depend on additional factors. Very simply, movement depends upon the attractiveness of the destination: we will travel further to visit a girlfriend or boyfriend than to visit an aunt or uncle. Equally, we are prepared to pay more on fares when shopping for new clothes, than when buying a magazine and we are also willing to spend more time travelling on a visit made occasionally (for example, to a dentist) than on regular trips (to, say, a hairdresser). In other words, every trip is some balance between the attractions of the destination, and the costs of getting there. These may be expressed as time, or effort, or expense, but together we can regard them as the FRICTION OF DISTANCE. We can illustrate this quite simply. Consider the examples of a football team, or a rock group. If they are not very good, we might be prepared to travel as far as the local ground, or the youth club, to see them. If they are more competent, then a visit to the next town might be worth while, and if they are excellent (say, a national team or internationally-famous stars), then an occasional trip to London would not be out of the question.

We can summarise this in the following way. In figure 1.2, we

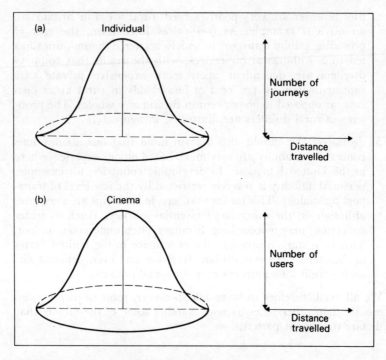

Figure 1.2   a) An individual's action cone
b) An action cone around a cinema or similar site

have a diagram of SPATIAL INTERACTION, or the way in which movement decreases with distance. The illustration can be interpreted in two ways. In figure 1.2(a), we have an interaction cone for an individual, who is located at the centre of the cone. As we can see, (s)he makes most trips locally, with occasional journeys over longer distances. Beyond a certain distance, no trips are made. This boundary will of course vary from individual to individual, in keeping with the factors determining personal mobility that we have already outlined. For an international businessman, the boundary may be a continent, while for an infirm pensioner it may be only the corner shop.

An alternative view is taken in figure 1.2(b), in which the centre of the cone represents a particular location, such as a shopping centre, a cinema or a school. Again, interaction falls away with distance, and the majority of the users live relatively close-by.

1.3 The measurement of distance decay

Although the distances over which people are prepared to travel vary, there are similarities in the general *shape* of the interaction cone; indeed this has been termed the fundamental law of geography, namely that interaction is always more powerful over short

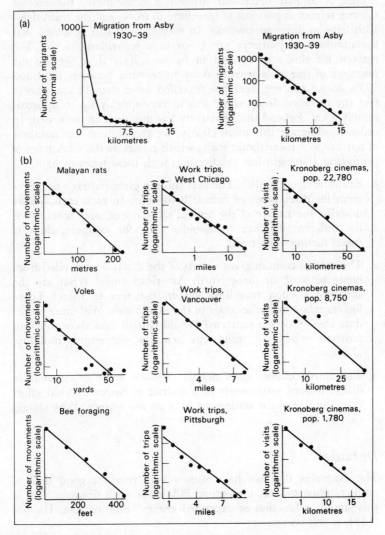

Figure 1.3   *a) Distance decay in migration, using normal and logarithmic scales*
       b) Nine examples of distance decay, all using logarithmic scales
       (Source: Haynes, 1974)

distances than long ones, which we in shorthand terms can call
DISTANCE DECAY.

What is particularly interesting about this principle is the way
in which very different types of interaction seem to result in very
similar patterns of behaviour. Figure 1.3(b) for example, provides
examples of three types of interaction; the first column provides
details of animal behaviour around a home base, the second
column relates to patterns of travelling to work, and the third deals
with trips to different cinemas. In each case, it will be noted that
the numbers of journeys are given in a logarithmic scale. The
reasons for this are revealed in figure 1.3(a). Here we see the
numbers of migrants leaving Asby in Sweden between 1930 and
1939. As we can see, very few travelled more than 15 km, and in
fact the distance decay effect sets in very quickly up to approximately 3 km. Beyond this, relatively few migrants are recorded. In
order to illustrate this more clearly, we can convert the numbers
of movers to a logarithmic scale, which possesses the advantage of
producing a straight-line relationship with these types of data.

1. Examine figure 1.3(b). The first column gives patterns of movement for three types of animal behaviour. In each case, briefly
   describe the nature of the animal's behaviour, and account for
   the different distance thresholds: why, for example, do rats
   travel further than bees?

2. The second column gives details of the distances travelled from
   home to work in three North American cities. What are the
   constraints upon travelling longer distances to work? These
   figures relate to studies done in the early 1960s. Will more recent
   data show different patterns? Would British data show different
   patterns? (Bear in mind our remarks concerning mobility,
   above.)

3. The third column gives details of visits made to cinemas in
   different-sized settlements in a district in Sweden. What effect
   does the size of the settlement have on attendance? Why should
   this occur?

Discussion

The examples that we have shown here reveal a good deal of
predictability, that is, interaction falls away with distance. Nor is
this simply a function of expended energy, time or cost. Haynes
(1974, p. 99) writes:

> It is interesting to note that the wind dispersal of seeds, pollen,
> and inert particles appears to follow a similar distribution . . . .
> Other physical patterns, such as the ground-level distribution of

sulphur dioxide concentration with distance from a power station chimney, or the intensity of fallout with distance from a nuclear test explosion, seem to be of the same type.

It is when we look at this distance decay relationship, that is repeated time and time again in very different contexts, that we can understand just why it has been referred to as the 'fundamental law' of geography.

1.4 The gravity model

The predictability of the distance decay relationship allows us to express it in a mathematical way. This was first done by Sir Isaac Newton, in his studies of the gravitational field of the planets, and as we shall see, has been applied in many other fields. Nonetheless, his original work has given to this work the name GRAVITY MODELLING. A simple equation might be

$$I = \frac{m_1 \times m_2}{d_{12}} \qquad [1]$$

Let us examine the terms in equation 1. First, I represents interaction. This is proportional to the size of two objects, which we can call m_1 and m_2. Newton used the term 'mass', but we can more easily think of them as two magnets. The larger and more powerful the magnets are, the more they will attract each other, and the greater the force – or interaction – between them will be. I will however also be influenced by the distance between m_1 and m_2; if they are too far apart, they will not be able to attract each other at all. We can illustrate this using iron filings, and figure 1.4 shows some experiments undertaken using different strengths of magnets which are different distances apart (McBride 1976, p. 25).

Once we have established these general principles of interaction, we can apply them to various geographical examples. A more usual form of the equation for the gravity model is given below:

$$I_{12} = \frac{P_1 P_2}{d_{12}} \qquad [2]$$

In equation 2, we are predicting the interaction between two settlements, of different populations, P. The interaction that we are considering is in the form of shopping trips, with people leaving settlement 1 (the smaller centre) to travel to settlement 2 (the larger centre, with better facilities). Naturally, when the two centres are large, then there are more people who will make shopping trips. Moreover, if P_2 is large, it will have more attractive shopping facilities than if it has only a small population. Consequently, as

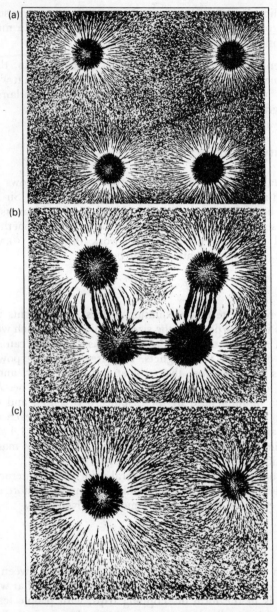

Figure 1.4   a) Four magnets, of equal strength, too far apart to attract each other;
b) four magnets, of equal strength, close enough to attract each other;
c) a strong and weak magnet
(Source: *McBride, 1976*)

P_1 and P_2 increase, then the interaction between them increases. As before however, the value of I_{12} will be scaled down by the distance between the two settlements.

At this point, we need to remind ourselves exactly what we can and cannot use a GRAVITY MODEL for. We *cannot* use it to predict the behaviour of a single individual or household; as we have seen, individuals vary in terms of their mobility. However, the gravity model is usually used to deal with hundreds, or more likely thousands of individual behaviour patterns. When this is done, the value of I that is produced represents an *average* value for interaction. We would expect differences as far as particular persons or households are concerned, as their distance decay patterns vary, owing to their own personal circumstances (income, age and so on). Nonetheless, the overall – or 'aggregate' – figure for interaction should be valuable.

The value of gravity models has been demonstrated in several contexts. Sophisticated developments of the ideas outlined here have been used in various fields, and below we outline two very different examples.

1. Employment around the third London airport
The fact that there exist predictable patterns of human behaviour is used by planners. They are able, for instance, to use the information on journey to work trips to make predictions about the results of possible developments. Figure 1.5 shows the results of such a prediction. In this case, the study examines the effects of the construction of the third London airport on a site at Thurleigh in Bedfordshire. Such a large development would involve approximately 65,000 jobs, and all these employees would of course require homes. Using gravity models, it is possible to forecast *where* these homes could best be located, and such a prediction is shown in figure 1.5(a).

Of course, this model needs to take into account other factors. These include:

1. Noise around the airport.
2. Good agricultural land.
3. Land of high landscape value.
4. Mineral deposits.

This information can be incorporated as constraints upon the location of the planned development, which gives the distribution shown in figure 1.5(b). Here the noise contours about the runway can clearly be seen, as can the fact that the residential development would be concentrated away from these areas.

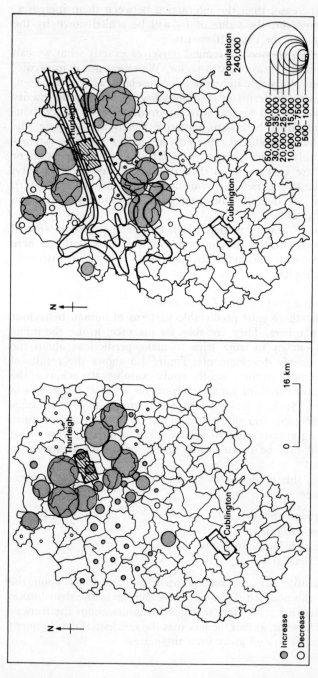

Figure 1.5(a)   Potential growth around Thurleigh; constraints of noise and agricultural land not taken into account (see text).

Figure 1.5(b)   Potential growth around Thurleigh; taking the constraints into account (Source: Foot, 1981).

2. *Archaeology in Cappadocia*

An entirely different application is revealed in figure 1.6, which shows predictions for the locations of 33 towns in Bronze Age Anatolia (now Turkey). No records of the location of the majority of these settlements have survived the last 4,000 years, although records indicate that a thriving trade did exist. Using a version of the gravity model, the geographers undertaking the research assumed that places mentioned most frequently in the records would be the largest settlements. Using that information, it is poss-

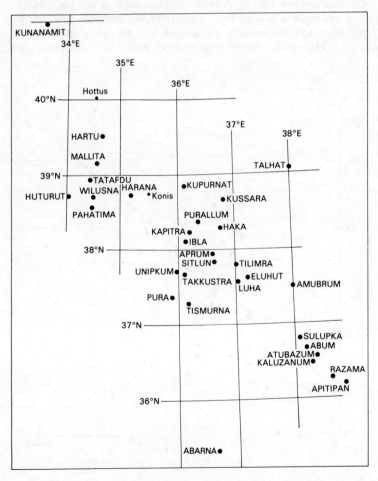

Figure 1.6   *Predictions for the location of thirty-three Bronze Age towns in Anatolia, using gravity model techniques (*Source: *Tobler and Wineburg, 1971)*

ible to make some predictions about the relative locations of pairs of towns known to have had trade links. Thus pairs of towns mentioned frequently together were probably close-by, while towns less frequently mentioned were probably distant.

The 'map' prediction in figure 1.6 is only a rough guide; all the locations are subject to an error of approximately 50 k. Nonetheless, this is a better means of choosing sites to investigate than simply looking for likely sites on the landscape or investigating traces of remains found by the public. (Unfortunately, the authors do not tell us whether any of the sites has yet been uncovered.)

Of course, the list of possible applications of simple gravity model concepts is a long one. An interesting example is given by Zipf, who was responsible for identifying the 'principle of least effort' (1949, p. 1). Over a period of time, he monitored the

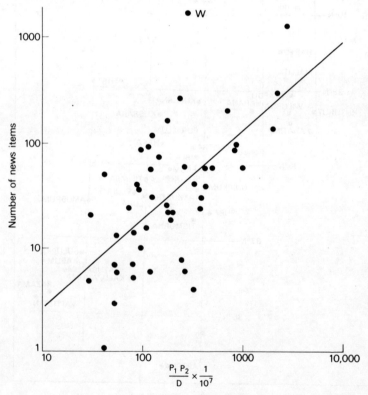

Figure 1.7   The relationship between the number of news items and the predicted value for 'information flow'. 'W' is the plotted position of Washington itself. (Source: Zipf, 1949)

contents of the *Washington Post,* and noted the origins of the stories that it carried. When he graphed the results, he noted a strong relationship between the distance from Washington to the location of the story, and the size of the location. In other words, the interaction (in this case, measured by flows of information between places) is proportional to the size of places, and scaled down by their distance away; an example is shown in figure 1.7.

1. Let us recreate Zipf's research. Over a one-week period, examine the contents of a selection of national newspapers (avoid the popular tabloids, where the news coverage is restricted). Note for each international story:
   (a) The location of the story (United States, Iran, etc.). For large countries (United States, Soviet Union) attempt to locate the report as precisely as possible.
   (b) The number of column inches attributed to each story.

2. At the end of the week, you should possess the following data:
   (a) A list of all the countries reported.
   (b) Their distance from London.
   (c) Their population.
   (d) The total length of column inches for each country.

3. You are now in a position to recreate Zipf's graph. For each country, you should work out an answer to the equation, solving for *I*:

$$I = \frac{P_1 P_2}{d_{1_2}} \qquad [3]$$

   where P_1 is the population of Britain; P_2 the population of the country reported; d_{1_2} the distance in miles or kilometres between them. The value of *I* that emerges represents 'information flow', although the units involved are artificial: we are only interested in the *relative* values of *I*.

4. Place this value on the graph, using values of *I* on the *X* axis, and column inches on the *Y* axis.

5. Examine the graph. Is there a consistent relationship between the predicted values of *I* and the column inches, which measure the actual information flow?

Discussion

This exercise illustrates the general principles of interaction between locations. Naturally enough, there will be some deviations from the general pattern, and we should ask ourselves why they occur. It may be useful to try to explain any deviations (that is more or fewer column inches than predicted) in terms of the following explanations:

1. 'Special' relationships, such as former colonial ties or the European Community.
2. 'Strategic' relationships, such as our dependence upon oil-producing countries.
3. 'Freak events', such as major natural or man-made disasters, which evoke international sympathy.

Do these results confirm or deny what has been called the fundamental law of geography? In other words, do we have a very ordered view of the world in which the movement of ideas (and goods, and people) is closely related to distance?

Key issues

MOBILITY A person's ability to move. The term can be used at a number of different scales, from day-to-day movements to long-distance ones, but the distance and the frequency with which an individual moves is related to that person's individual circumstances.

SPATIAL INTERACTION Movements between locations in space are essential and, in general, the overall pattern of the thousands of individual shopping trips or journeys to work is predictable. Most people will expend the least effort in order to fulfil a certain aim; many aims require only very short trips and few necessitate longer journeys. In a similar way, the interaction around a certain location in space (a shopping centre for example) is predictable; most interaction is with users located close to the shopping centre and there is little interaction with places much further afield. The actual extent of this interaction, or the boundary beyond which no interaction with the shopping centre takes place, depends on the size of the shopping centre as well as the mobility of the people living in the area.

FRICTION OF DISTANCE In order to get from A to B, an effort has to be made to overcome the distance between them. The journey takes time and/or costs money, and this may deter the individual from making the trip. The greater the distance, the greater is this 'friction'.

DISTANCE DECAY This is an important geographical term which refers to the general overall pattern of spatial interaction, that interaction falls away with increasing distance. It is worth while to note that this rule has a very wide applicability. There is a clear distance decay effect produced by pollution settling around a factory chimney, the noise produced by a pneumatic drill, the destruction around the epicentre of an earthquake and the movement of sand grains by the wind.

GRAVITY MODELS When a phenomenon is as predictable as spatial interaction appears to be, it can usually be expressed very neatly as a mathematical relationship. A gravity model expresses the interaction between two locations in space as being proportional to the size of the two locations (using the assumption that the size of a settlement or shopping centre will be a measure of its power of attraction) and inversely proportional to the distance between them (this part of the formula incorporating the distance decay effect). Thus the gravity model expresses in a shorthand (mathematical) way a fundamental geographical relationship and the formula is used, in modified terms by planners in a variety of fields.

2
Interaction and location

2.1 Action spaces

In Chapter 1 we examined the ways in which behaviour patterns conform to certain norms. One finding which consistently emerges is that there are limits to interaction; in other words, there are boundaries beyond which we rarely go. These boundaries are not rigid, of course. They are elastic, and the more mobile we are, the further we can push them back.

We can term the areas within these boundaries an *activity* or ACTION SPACE. This implies that this is the geographical extent of our normal, daily business.

1. On a sketch map of your local area, pinpoint the most important locations – or *'Stations'* as they are sometimes called. These will include:
   (*a*) Home.
   (*b*) School.
   (*c*) Friends' homes.
   (*d*) Shops.
   (*e*) Recreation – disco, cinema, pool.

2. Draw a boundary around the usual, *daily* action space.

3. Compare the boundaries of other individuals; try, for example,
   (*a*) Older students.
   (*b*) Younger students.
   (*c*) Parents or teachers.

Attempt to explain variations in the extent of the daily action spaces. Is there any relationship between size and age, for example?

Discussion

This simple exercise illustrates that we each have an action space. They will vary geographically, as they centre around our homes and our work; they will tend to be of similar size for people who are equally mobile, and more extensive for those who are more mobile.

2.2 The good, the bad and the ugly

Within the action space of any individual, there are however more than the 'stations' to consider. We can also take into account the 'goods' and the 'bads'; those factors which improve or upset our lives.

1. Mark on your sketch map all the 'bads'; for example, all the main roads that are noisy and/or dangerous, any derelict buildings, any factories that are noisy or dirty, and any other location that impinges upon the quality of your daily life.

2. Now, repeat the exercise, but this time concentrate upon the 'goods'; the recreational areas, the library, any shops, even any attractive views (either urban or rural).

3. Now attempt to 'score' your action space, using the following scheme:

   +2 very desirable ⎤
   +1 desirable   ⎦ the goods
   _____
   −1 undesirable   ⎤
   −2 very undesirable⎦ the bads

   For each thing you have identified, give it a score, and then produce a total for the action space as a whole: divide this total by the number of goods and bads to give a final score somewhere between −2 and +2 (to one decimal place).

4. Compare the scores. When you look at all the individual action spaces of people in your class, are there distinct patterns, with some areas showing overall positive values (suggesting that they are desirable) and others showing overall negative values (indicating undesirability)?

Discussion

This exercise shows that each action space contains a mixture of goods and bads, and that in some cases, the goods might outweigh the bads, and that in others, the opposite may apply. Of course, it is likely that your views may differ from those who have a similar action space to yours – they may have emphasised different things, and even scored the same things differently. For example, you have probably not included your school, although for people who live nearby, it is probably a 'bad', due to noise, cars being parked, and litter being dropped. Similarly, a factory may be noisy and dirty, or a source of scarce employment. Consequently, an individual's score will depend on his or her circumstances.

Because of these problems of subjectivity, we need to approach such questions in a different way.

2.3 Externalities

The 'goods' and 'bads' can also be considered as EXTERNALITIES. These have been described in the following way (Johnston 1979, pp. 7–8):

> Most of the facilities used in everyday life are available at certain places only, and travel is necessary to obtain the required components of the level of social wellbeing. Some people, because of where they live, are closer to parks and precincts, to shops and offices, doctors and dentists, fire and police stations: travel to these costs time and money, and the less that has to be spent, the better off people are. All of the facilities used do not produce positive externalities, however; it may be pleasant to live next to a park, but not to a sewerage works or to an odorous factory.
>
> Where one lives within the built environment with respect to positive and negative externalities can have a major influence on wellbeing. Not surprisingly, there is conflict to live in the 'better' areas, and, since this conflict is mediated in the property market, where ability to pay is the major determinant of success, the richer and more powerful are able to reserve those better areas for themselves.

From Johnston's remarks, we can see that externalities are far more straightforward than our rather vague terms 'goods' and 'bads'. You will remember from our example of a school that one 'facility', as Johnston calls them, can at one and the same time be both a 'good' and a 'bad' to different people (it may even be a 'good' or a 'bad' to the same student on different days). We can, however, incorporate these ideas quite easily using the externality approach.

Figure 2.1(a) illustrates the costs and benefits of a motorway to people at different locations; in other words the same facility can act as both a positive and a negative externality, depending upon the location of the individual in relation to it.

The motorway is located at point X. The vertical axis measures two things. The first is the costs imposed by the road on those who live nearby. These can be measured in money terms, as they relate to things like the cost of double-glazing. Naturally enough, these *disbenefits* decrease quite quickly as one gets further away from the road; indeed, by the time X1 is reached, the effects of noise and pollution are negligible. The second is the *benefits* that can be gained by residents using the motorway. These are also measured in

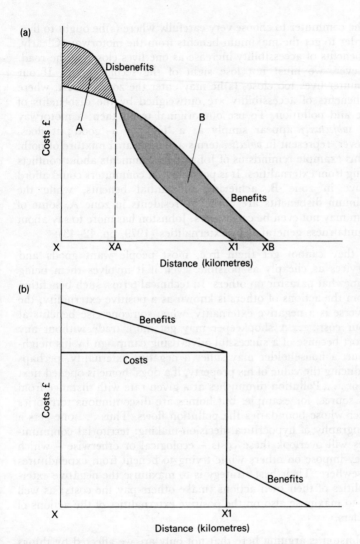

Figure 2.1   *a)*   *The relationship between benefits and disbenefits with*
distance from a major road (Source: *Wheeler, 1976*)
b)   *The relationship between benefits and disbenefits with distance*
from a swimming pool (Source: *Smith, 1977*)

money terms, relating to savings in fuel and time. These savings
also decrease with distance, disappearing at *XB*.

Figure 2.1(a) shows two things, therefore. The first is the way
in which both the benefits and the disbenefits display the now
familiar distance decay pattern. This means that it is important

for the commuter to choose very carefully where (s)he ought to live, in order to get the maximum benefits from the motorway. Clearly, the benefits of accessibility increase as one lives closer to the road. However, we must not lose sight of the second point. If our commuter lives too close, (s)he may enter the zone X–XA, where the benefits of accessibility are outweighed by the disbenefits of noise and pollution. To use our original terms then, a motorway may *subjectively* appear simply as a 'bad' or a 'good'; it does, however, represent in *objective* terms a complicated mixture of both.

This example reminds us of Johnston's comments about conflicts arising from externalities. It is possible that commuters could afford to live in zone B, achieving substantial benefits, while the maximum disbenefits are borne by residents in zone A, some of whom may not even be car-owners. Johnston has more to say about the unfairness generated by externalities (1979, pp. 42–43):

> If they cannot get them free, most people want goods and services as cheaply as possible, even if it involves them being somewhat parasitic on others. In technical terms, such benefiting from the actions of others is known as a positive externality; the reverse is a negative externality, when someone else benefits at your cost . . .. A shopkeeper may get more trade without any effort because of a successful advertising campaign by his neighbour; a householder may suffer a negative externality, perhaps reducing the value of his property, if a dogs' home is opened next door . . .. Pollution diminishes at a given rate with distance from its source, for example, but homes are discontinuous territories over whose boundaries the pollution flows. Thus . . . one gets a geography of hypocritical decision-making: territorial communities will overlook these costs – ecological or otherwise – which they impose on others while trying to benefit from expenditures elsewhere. Their best strategy is to maximise the negative externalities of their own actions (make others pay the costs) as well as to maximise also on the positive externalities of the actions of others.

Johnston is arguing here that not only are we affected by things over which we have no control, but that we also affect each other by our actions. Furthermore, because homes are small (discontinuous) units of land, individuals have little power to resist some negative externalities. Johnston's example implies that a factory could pollute a wide area, for which it bears none of the costs; these costs are passed on to individuals living in the polluted area.

Nor are industries the only culprits in this 'hypocritical' game. Our local authorities, too, try to minimise their expenditures, by encouraging the use of others' facilities. Residents in suburban or rural areas can use libraries or recreational sites in towns, without necessarily paying the additional annual costs that the urban rate-payers have to bear. This is shown in figure 2.1(b). Here we have a swimming bath, located at X. This is paid for by the residents of the local authority, which extends out to X1. As far as benefits are concerned, these are distributed in a distance decay manner; those living close by have an obvious advantage, and may in fact go swimming more frequently. Beyond X1, these benefits of prox-imity diminish but they are replaced by the ability to use the baths 'on the cheap'. These suburbanites can swim for the cost of entry, without paying anything towards the real costs which are borne by the ratepayers in the local authority area where the baths are.

Of course, our urban dwellers may get their own back. They can site their rubbish tips out in rural areas, much to the chagrin of the latter, as we shall see below.

2.4 The measurement of externalities

The graphs shown above suggest that we can in fact measure externalities and their impact quite precisely. Indeed, for planning purposes, and in situations where compensation is to be awarded, rigorous measurement of the intensity and extent of an externality's influence is vital.

This does not imply that it is difficult to undertake such a meas-urement. Bale, for example, has studied the effects of football grounds on nearby populations (Bale 1980, p. 93):

> In the immediate neighbourhood of football grounds, several nuisances are generated which are unwillingly 'consumed' by local residents. Questions raised at a meeting of Leicester City Council in 1978 led to a report suggesting action to alleviate the distress suffered by local residents, particularly those whose homes are in close proximity to Leicester City football ground at Filbert Street, from the disturbance caused by persons on their way to and from football matches. Complaints from residents include abuse, damage to property, smells (from hot dog sellers) and nervous stress. Such was the degree of vandalism around Derby County's ground in 1976 that local residents sought legal advice on getting the game banned. In the New Cross areas of London, the Hatcham Park Residents' Association is actively opposing the activities of Millwall Foot-ball Club.

He then goes on to show how these feelings can be measured in a geographic context (1980, p. 94):

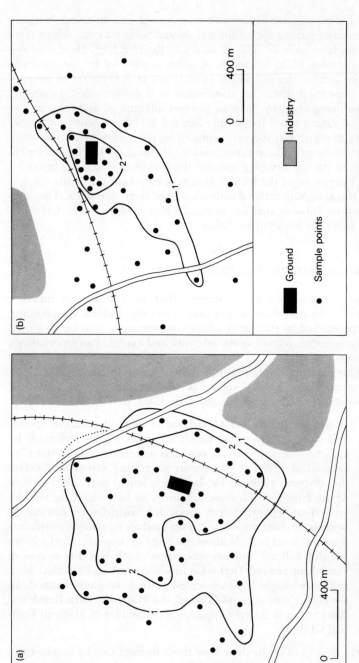

Figure 2.2   Externality fields around two football grounds: (a) Derby County and (b) Charlton Athletic (Source: Bale, 1980)

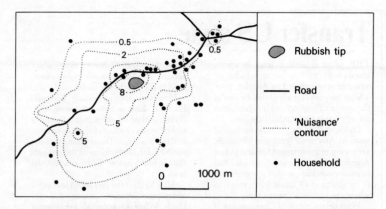

*Figure 2.3   The distribution of externality or nuisance contours around a rubbish tip in Tenhola (*Source: *Löytönen and Löytönen, 1980)*

The nuisance fields of two clubs, Derby County and Charlton Athletic, are shown [in figure 2.2]. These were constructed by asking a sample of residents near each ground whether they found the club 'a severe nuisance', 'a nuisance', or 'no nuisance at all'. Sample points were then given a score of 2, 1 or 0 respectively, and nuisance contours interpolated. As expected, there was a distance decay effect, and in both cases, the nuisance field was concentrated spatially.

Figure 2.2 shows quite clearly how a *nuisance* or *externality field* can be constructed. A somewhat more sophisticated example is shown in figure 2.3. This shows the externality field around a municipal rubbish tip in Tenhola, a small rural municipality in southwestern Finland. The researchers conducted a questionnaire survey which asked the respondents whether they were troubled by the following nuisances: noise, traffic, litter, smells, smoke, rats, birds, flies, spoiling of the landscape, pollution of surface waters, pollution of subsoil and 'anti-social persons'. On the basis of numerical scores given to each of these nuisance factors a map was constructed to show the overall disadvantage caused by the dumping ground. Once again, the distance decay effect is clear, and it is interesting to note that the researchers found that neither the topography of the area nor the quality of the vegetation around the dumping ground had much effect on the pattern.

Discussion

Both these examples show how externality fields can be defined, although for the sake of simplicity only the disbenefits have been

Transfer US style

THE most expensive trial in sports history—$5 million so far—kicks off again next month in Los Angeles, after a hung jury and an allegation by one of the sports administrators involved, that the other side had nobbled the jury.

Oakland Raiders, the most successful team in American (grid-iron) football, are trying to move from Oakland to Los Angeles, a manoeuvre which has become familiar in US professional team sports of all kinds (they move to where the spectators are richer).

With this in mind Al Davis, owner of the Raiders, wants to transplant the team from Oakland, an impoverished urban sprawl across the bay from San Francisco, to Los Angeles, the most populous county in the United States and one of the richest markets in the world. And since LA recently lost its

team, the Rams, to its even richer white suburb of Anaheim 60 miles away, Raider Davis aches to fill the void.

However, the governing National Football League refused permission, claiming that its rules only allowed a move from a city to its suburbs, not one city to another, so Davis promptly sued the NFL for $160 million on the grounds that it had violated Federal anti-trust laws.

After 55 days the jury failed to reach a unanimous verdict, voting 8–2 for Davis. When it was revealed that one of the two "hold outs" lived in Anaheim, Davis claimed he had been planted on the jury by the NFL. On the other hand, the NFL claims it cannot expect a fair trial in LA. Davis says that it's "the law of the jungle."

Figure 2.4   This press report shows that locational factors are important to American football teams, which 'move to where the spectators are richer': the Rangers have in fact now moved to LA

measured. As we should now expect, both clearly show distance – decay properties, and it has proved possible to delimit zones which we have termed 'negative externality' or 'nuisance' fields. These zones could have considerable practical importance in helping local authorities, for example, to decide upon the location of certain facilities which are likely to generate a nuisance to local residents. In both studies we have described, the researchers have concluded by making proposals that would reduce or even eliminate the nuisance to individual households. Bale's suggestion, concerning the nuisance generated by football grounds, is to suburbanise British football: in other words to encourage football clubs to change the location of their grounds from predominantly central city sites to suburban sites as part of modern, planned sports complexes with adequate car parking and other facilities. As figure 2.4 shows, this trend is already well advanced in the United States. In the case of the dumping ground, the Finnish health authorities already recommend a 'protecting zone' around all municipal rubbish tips of between 500 to 1,000 m radius. The research revealed that the nuisances caused by the dump (particularly rats, flies and smoke) extended as far as 2 km away and the authors concluded that the 'protecting zone', to be effective, needs to have a radius of between 1,500–2,000 m.

2.5 Externalities and residential preference

In the above discussion, we have concentrated very much upon *objective* measurement; nonetheless, there is a good deal of evidence that many people have a clear understanding of not only nuisances, but also the fact that many facilities can act both as negative *and* positive externalities. In the following exercise, we aim to simulate the RESIDENTIAL LOCATION decision-making process, taking into account not only housing, but many other aspects of the urban environment.

1. Examine the list below of the five types of urban facilities (table 2.1).

2. Decide which ones you regard as being on balance *positive* externalities, and which ones you regard as generally *negative*. Be prepared to give a reason for each choice.

3. Group the externalities together in terms of whether you would like them in:
   (a) The same street as your home.
   (b) The next street.
   (c) The same neighbourhood.
   (d) The same town, but a different neighbourbood.
   (e) Somewhere out of town.
   Naturally, you will want the mainly positive facilities close by, and the mainly negative facilities further away.

Discussion

Examine your locational choices. How consistent are your views with those of your fellow students, and what might account for any dissimilarities? Naturally, those of you who follow football might like a ground close by; others might like the disruption to be contained further away.

Generally, the tendency is for everyone to want any facility that might have any negative aspects whatsoever to be located on someone else's doorstep. This is shown in figure 2.5, which gives the results of an American study. Nothing is required in the same street (block), and only a park is viewed as desirable on the next street. Many facilities which are ostensibly desirable are relegated to a good distance away; for example, it might be reassuring to have a fire station next door, but the sound of sirens would soon become very wearing. More predictably, all the obviously undesirable activities, such as prisons and dumps, are wished well away. Johnston is, of course, right to call this hypocritical; no community can survive without sewage treatment, and no prisoner is likely to

Table 2.1   Externalities in urban areas

Group of facilities	Example	Same street	Next street	Same neighbourhood	Other neighbourhood	Out of town
Entertainment	1 Park					
	2 Theatre					
	3 Museum					
	4 Cinema					
	5 Bingo hall					
	6 Sports ground					
Utilities	7 Fire station					
	8 Police station					
	9 Bus station					
	10 Rail station					
	11 Shopping precinct					
	12 Market					
	13 Library					
	14 Tip					
	15 Sewage plant					
Health and Social services	16 Health centre					
	17 Hospital					
	18 Mental Hospital					
	19 Prison					
	20 Borstal					
	21 Vagrants' hostel					
	22 Funeral directors					
	23 Nursing home					
Education	24 Primary school					
	25 Secondary school					
	26 College					
	27 Family planning clinic					
Housing and employment	28 High-rise flats					
	29 Caravan park					
	30 Offices					
	31 Factories					

(*Source*: Smith, 1980)

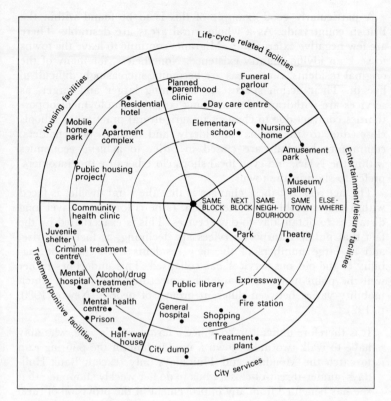

Figure 2.5   Preferred residential distance from different public facilities (Source: Smith, 1980)

stay for long in the vicinity of a prison even if (s)he did escape. Nonetheless, it is perhaps not surprising that the wealthy choose to live well away from any potential threats, leaving undesirable areas for those who have not the financial means to make their perfect locational choice.

2.6 Resumé: action spaces, externalities and the quality of life

Throughout this chapter, we have tended to concentrate upon the most dramatic aspects of externalities, the phenomena that deserve the name 'nuisances'. However, this should not blind us to the fact that our QUALITY OF LIFE is determined – on a day-to-day basis – far more by the quiet, unspectacular and constant changes going on within our action spaces.

A particularly good example of this is to be found within the British countryside. As a whole, rural areas are desirable. There are few negative externalities. Migrants continue to leave the towns to seek an idyllic country existence. Nonetheless, for many of the original residents, rural areas are becoming increasingly difficult to live in. Their action spaces are becoming larger and larger, as services are withdrawn due to rising costs, as employment opportunities contract due to changes in agricultural practice, as schools close due to the influx of elderly and retired householders, community hospitals are closed in order to achieve economies within the NHS, and even local shops close because the 'incomers' prefer to shop in the towns.

The net result of these changes is that the rural dweller is faced with a major problem of interaction; (s)he is forced to travel long distances to obtain day-to-day services. This is exacerbated by the fact that public transport services are declining; as fuel costs rise, and as large numbers of the new residents have cars, the viability of the old bus services has collapsed. This underlines rather well the point made in Chapter 1, concerning the ways in which mobility varies between different groups of people (Newby 1980, p. 192):

> It is therefore difficult to convince a farmworker's wife, who may have to walk two miles down a muddy lane in the pouring rain to catch the Mondays and Thursdays only (except Bank Holidays) under-threat-of-closure bus to do her weekly shopping, that she has benefited from any improvement in the provision of rural amenities, when her access to them is increasingly denied.

> It is with this picture, repeated in Ambridges up and down the country, in mind that has caused a geographer to identify accessibility as 'the rural challenge', and Howard Newby himself to question the existence of 'a green and pleasant land'.

Key Issues

ACTION SPACE The pattern of our activity in space conforms to certain 'rules' or norms. Our normal day-to-day business takes us out of our homes and necessitates interaction with other locations. The size of the area in which we interact on a day-to-day basis – the spatial extent of our interaction – depends upon our mobility, but in each case we can define the boundaries to this area, and we can call this area our daily action space. In a similar way, we could identify our weekly, monthly or even yearly action space; the latter would include holidays which might involve trips abroad.

EXTERNALITIES There are phenomena in our environment, both natural and man-made, which affect the quality of our lives. These can be interpreted by us to be positive, if we consider them to be 'good', or negative if we feel their effect is 'bad'. Since these phenomena are external to, and outside our control (they are there whether we like them or not), they are referred to as 'externalities'. The area which is measurably affected by an externality is known as the externality field.

A crucial point to note concerning externalities is that we usually try to maximise the benefits of positive externalities to ourselves whilst trying to minimise the effects of negative externalities, often even at the expense of others. We are happy to support a by-pass round our own house, despite the fact that it takes the traffic off to annoy someone else.

THE QUALITY OF LIFE A person would probably begin to describe the 'quality' of his or her life by referring to the type of work (s)he has – whether it is dull or interesting, paid well or badly, the number of 'perks' and so on – and to other factors, such as the choice of friends and acquaintances, often considered to be within that person's control. If a person's job is ruining his or her quality of life, it may be fairly easy to change it. The problem, of course, is that in reality there are other constraints on our actions, and our everyday lives are conditioned to a greater or lesser degree by things *beyond our control*; we cannot always choose who our neighbours are! We have used the term 'quality of life' with this particular meaning in mind, that a person is conditioned by his or her location to suffer or to benefit from negative or positive externalities, as the case may be.

It should also be emphasised that a person's personal circumstances, which affect his or her mobility, are a vital consideration. In the context of rural Britain we have seen that the quality of life varies enormously depending on access to a motor car.

RESIDENTIAL LOCATION When a person decides to move house (s)he must make a series of decisions affecting the location of his or her new home. It is probable that people involved in this decision-making process have quite a clear idea of the type of house or flat, the setting and the location that would be most desirable to them. In reality, however, the majority of people compromise and relatively few people actually achieve their 'dream house' in the perfect location. The reason for this is that some people are able to purchase their homes whereas others are not; furthermore, within the group of actual or potential owner-occupiers, some people are more able to afford desirable housing in desirable areas, than are others.

Thus, within the constraints we all operate under – whether to do with our mobility or to do with the price of houses and what we can afford – we will tend to seek a residential location that combines the maximum benefits of positive externalities and the minimum disbenefits from negative externalities.

3
Migration and relocation

3.1 The causes of migration

In Chapter 2 we concentrated very much upon *daily* activity patterns in which all outward movements are retraced at the end of the day. There are of course also many examples of long-distance movements, in which the mover usually resettles in a permanent new home after the journey: for these types of moves, we usually reserve the name MIGRATION.

Any consideration of migration must start with an attempt at explanation. In our (daily) examples in Chapter 2, interaction was easily explained in terms of movements to work, or to shops, or other simple tasks. Migratory interaction is more complicated. First, we have to explain why people leave an area in which they or their families may have lived for many years, and second, we have to account for their choice of destination and relocation.

Historically, the bulk of migration throughout the world has been *from* rural areas *to* urban areas. As we showed in section 2.6, the countryside can be an exceptionally difficult place in which to live, even in a prosperous society such as our own. In addition to the problem of accessibility to services, there also exist very restricted employment opportunities (Newby 1980, p. 124):

> Employment opportunities for school leavers in rural areas are usually highly limited and their choice is often further circum-scribed by a lack of personal mobility. A job on the land is there-fore regarded as a handy stop-gap until the possession of a driving-licence opens up a much wider labour market, both geographically and occupationally. On average, a 16-year-old recruit to farming will have moved on by the age of 23.

Poor job opportunities here clearly constitute a PUSH FACTOR, although as Howard Newby shows, similar problems have over the last 150 years literally pushed people off the land (1980, pp. 124–125):

> In remoter rural areas, where agriculture has traditionally held a virtual monopoly of employment opportunities, the declining

demand for labour in agriculture has historically led to widespread rural depopulation. Former farmworkers have felt the need to move out to the towns and cities, in search not only of employment, but also of higher pay, better working conditions and increased opportunities for personal advancement; and farmers have felt the need to shed labour as an accompaniment to increasing productivity. This is, of course, no new process; rural depopulation first became identified as a social problem in the middle of the last century. On occasions rural depopulation has aroused considerable public concern and has even been represented as a draining away of the nation's life blood, to the detriment of the national character and vigour. However, an evaluation of rural depopulation needs to take account of a whole variety of factors. Undoubtedly, the people left behind can experience immense dislocation, amounting in extreme cases to complete social and economic dereliction, but with no economic base to support a larger rural population, conditions would have been worse if those who moved to the towns had chosen to remain in the countryside. Many who moved were glad to do so and the economy as a whole has benefited from the release of agricultural labour to take up employment in the expanding manufacturing and service sectors. The conventional wisdom has been that those who left the countryside were energetic and intelligent, leaving only a residue of the old and the inert, but we also ought to note that the urban view has often been the exact opposite; that the towns have received the rural dregs – the drifters, the shiftless, the workshy, the unattached flotsam of agricultural change. There is in fact no hard evidence to show that rural depopulation has been *socially* selective either way.

As we can see therefore, it is relatively easy to understand why people leave a particular area. It is however not easy to predict where migrants will finish their journeys. Their choice of destination of course depends upon the PULL FACTORS that different localities exert; however, these factors will often depend upon word-of-mouth descriptions and other secondary sources. The settlement of the interior of the United States has been described as being the result of 'illusions'; 'much of the heart of the North American continent was neglected by early settlers because of the absence of trees. European experience suggested that treeless land was also infertile' (Chapman 1979, p. 29). As Chapman also points out, the name 'Greenland' was a deliberate attempt to attract Viking immigrants to a country without many obvious pull factors.

The migration process is thus a complicated one to understand, although it is relatively easy to measure, as the next example shows.

3.2 Migration to an expanding nineteenth century town

By the late nineteenth century, rural – urban migration had already transformed the population map of Britain, with the coalfield-based northern industrial towns expanding rapidly, and the agricultural hinterlands suffering depopulation. Towns not on the coalfields were also experiencing growth and as an illustration we shall take Northampton, a prosperous light industrial centre (producing notably boots and shoes) and market town in the East Midlands.

Figure 3.1 consists of two maps, both of which show the place of birth of residents of Kingsthorpe according to the 1871 census. Kingsthorpe, now part of the built-up area of Northampton, was then an expanding suburb just to the north of Northampton itself. Two-thirds of its total population of 1,830 had been born in Kings-thorpe, but the remaining third originated from a variety of locations, from Northampton (4.5 per cent), elsewhere in the county of Northamptonshire (11.5 per cent), or elsewhere in the country (18.1 per cent). Figure 3.1(a) shows the precise location of county migrants and figure 3.1(b) shows the origins of the country-wide migrants.

1. With reference to figure 3.1(a):
   (*a*) Describe the pattern. Does it conform to the 'fundamental geographical law' that is, distance decay (see figure 1.3(a))?
   (*b*) Suggest an explanation for the migration pattern you have described.

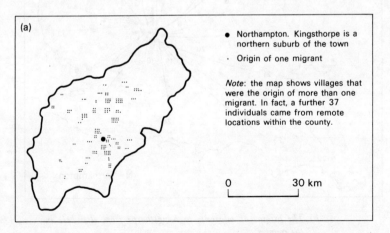

(a)

● Northampton. Kingsthorpe is a northern suburb of the town

· Origin of one migrant

Note: the map shows villages that were the origin of more than one migrant. In fact, a further 37 individuals came from remote locations within the county.

0   30 km

Figure 3.1   a) The origins of migrants to Kingsthorpe within Northamptonshire, 1871

(b)	County	Number of migrants		County	Number of migrants
1	Lancashire	12	14	Essex	1
2	Yorkshire	1	15	Hertfordshire	1
3	Lincolnshire	5	16	Bedfordshire	27
4	Nottinghamshire	1	17	Huntingdonshire	8
5	Staffordshire	13	18	Buckinghamshire	35
6	Shropshire	1	19	Oxfordshire	6
7	Herefordshire	2	20	Gloucestershire	1
8	Warwickshire	10	21	Glamorgan	1
9	Leicestershire	26	22	Cornwall	1
10	Rutland	3	23	Devon	5
11	Cambridgeshire	1	24	Hampshire	2
12	Norfolk	2	25	Surrey	4
13	Suffolk	1	26	Kent	5

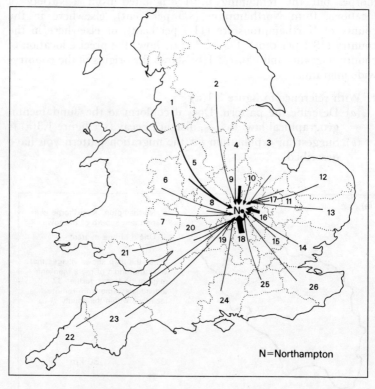

N=Northampton

b) *The origins of migrants to Kingsthorpe from elsewhere in the country*

(c) Although you may have decided that the overall pattern is a predictable one, how easy would it have been to predict the destination of each individual migrant shown on the map?

2. Attempt to answer Questions (a) and (b) above, for figure 3.1(b). Question (c) can be slightly modified for figure 3.1(b). Would it have been more, or less, difficult to predict the actual destination of individual country-wide migrants compared to the county migrants in 1871?

Table 3.1   Place of Birth of Residents of Kingsthorpe (1871 census)

(a)	Kingsthorpe	1,220
	Northampton	85
	County of Northamptonshire	332
	Country (except Northamptonshire)	190
	Abroad	3

(b) *County*:

Buckinghamshire	35	Hampshire	2
Bedfordshire	27	Herefordshire	2
Leicestershire	26	Norfolk	2
London	15	Cambridgeshire	1
Lancashire	13	Cornwall	1
Staffordshire	13	Essex	1
Warwickshire	0	Glamorgan	1
Huntingdonshire	8	Gloucestershire	1
Oxfordshire	6	Hertfordshire	1
Devon	5	Nottinghamshire	1
Kent	5	Shropshire	1
Lincolnshire	5	Suffolk	1
Surrey	4	Yorkshire	1
Rutland	3		

Note: These are the old counties prior to local government reorganisation

Discussion

In the second half of the nineteenth century, rural depopulation had become well established, for the reasons identified above in the quotation by H. Newby; farms were shedding labour and in any case wages were low compared with the new jobs obtainable in the towns and cities. Villages were losing people, whereas towns were growing quickly. The pattern shown in figure 3.1(a) indicates a distance decay function at work, with the majority of within-county migrants to Kingsthorpe coming from not-too-distant rural locations. Indeed, as one moves northward from Northampton, one approaches other urban settlements, notably Leicester; the attraction of Northampton decreases as the attraction of Leicester increases. The general pattern of migration to Kingsthorpe is therefore predictable and this distance decay function is even clearer when figure 3.1(b) is examined – the vast majority of immigrants come from neighbouring counties.

However, it should be clear from an example such as this that although the *general* migration pattern to Kingsthorpe is predictable, there is no specific rule that we can apply to *individuals* who have chosen to migrate in relation to their destination. So, although it is not surprising that a majority of country-wide migrants to Kingsthorpe originated from neighbouring counties not too far away, it would be wrong to infer that we could have predicted that any individual from the thousands of migrants (from, say, rural Buckinghamshire) would have chosen Kingsthorpe as a destination.

3.3 Inter-continental migrations

Although we have varied the spatial scale of our discussion, we have as yet barely touched upon the major migration waves that have occurred throughout the world. Few, if any nations existing today can claim a racial 'purity' that has not been enriched by successive waves of migration. Primary school history books contain numerous events that testify to these movements: the Great Wall of China, built two millenia ago to keep out the Mongol armies; the Battle of Hastings (1066) and the Norman invasion of Britain; 1492 and the first steps towards the colonisation of North America. An even better example is that of the Zulu Wars in Southern Africa in the late nineteenth century, which represented the head-on collision of *two* migrating nations, the Dutch Boers from South Africa, heading north, and the Zulu nations, heading south.

As with other migrations, the basic laws of interaction still apply – in other words, for migration to take place over long distances, the pull factors have to be very great, and the push factors large enough to disrupt the population. This principle emerges quite clearly in figure 3.2, which illustrates the three great waves of migration that were directed at the United States over the last 150 years.

1. The first wave of immigration came from Ireland. List the push factors which produced this movement, and suggest the attractions of the United States for the Irish.

2. The second and quantitatively biggest influx came from eastern Europe and Russia. Who constituted this group, what problems

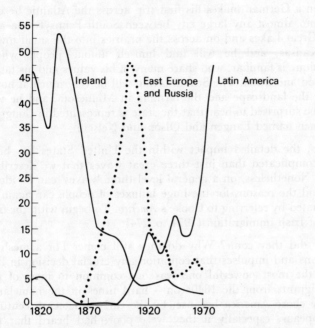

Figure 3.2   Immigration into the United States, percentages entering from different areas, 1920–70 (after Haggett). Note that the data are in proportions, and that total numbers of immigrants decline dramatically after the First World War

did they face in Europe, and what were the attractions of the United States for them?

3. The third contemporary immigration has as its origins Latin America. What prompts this movement, and where do the migrants go within the United States?

Discussion

The migration of millions of people over thousands of miles from their varied homelands to the new land of America remains one of the most spectacular manifestations of intercontinental population movement. The people who now call themselves American are descendants of immigrants from dozens of different countries in Asia, Africa and Europe and most recently South America; it is worth while remembering that the chances of an American being directly of English stock are less than one in four. As Alistair Cooke has said (1974, p. 273):

Only the English visitor is still surprised by this palpable fact.

When a German makes his first trip across the Atlantic he can go into almost any large city between South Pennsylvania and the Great Lakes and on across the prairies into the small towns of Kansas, and he will find himself among people whose physique is familiar, who share many of his values and his tastes in food and drink. The Scandinavian will be very much at home with the landscape and the farming in Minnesota, and he will not be surprised to hear that the state is represented in Congress by men named Langen and Olson and Nelsen.

Thus, the detailed impact within the United States has been more complicated than just three great waves that we described above. Nonetheless, on a general level three 'waves' can be ident- ified and the reasons for the huge influxes of people can again be illuminated by referring to Cooke's *America*. To begin with, the first wave of Irish immigration (1974, p. 274):

Why did they come? Why do they still come? For a mesh of reasons and impulses that condition any crucial decision in life. But the most powerful one was one common to most of the immigrants from the 1840s on – hard times in the homeland. They chose America because, by the early nineteenth century, Europeans, especially if they were poor, had heard that the Americans had had a revolution that successfully overthrew the old orders of society. Madame de Staël could tell a Boston scholar, in 1817, 'You are the advance guard of the human race.' And Goethe, ten years later, wrote for anybody to read: 'Amerika, du hast es besser als unser Kontinent' (which may be loosely translated as 'America, you have things better over there'). He was thinking of the freedom from this binding force of 'useless traditions'. But people who had never heard of Madame de Staël and Goethe picked up the new belief that there was a green land far away preserved 'from robbers, knights and ghosts affrighting'. Whenever life could hardly be worse at home, they came to believe that life was better in America.

In Ireland in the middle 1840s human life had touched bottom. Ironically, two causes of the Irish plight came from America. The rising competition of American agriculture made thousands of very small farmers (300,000 of Ireland's 685,000 farms had less than three acres) shift from tillage to grazing, on barren ground. And the potato blight, which was to putrefy vast harvests in a few weeks, had crossed the Atlantic from America in 1845. Within five years the potato famine had claimed almost a million Irish lives, over twenty thousand of them dropping in the fields from starvation.

In the 1840s and 1850s about 1,700,000 Irish migrated to

America, which amounted to nearly a quarter of the pre-famine Irish population. As Cooke concludes 'Hunger, then, was the spur in Ireland'. For the second wave of immigration hunger was not the 'push factor'. Throughout Europe political and religious persecution was providing certain groups of people with the reason to make the dramatic choice to migrate. The group most affected in terms of both the strength of the discrimination and the numbers involved were the Jewish communities in Germany, Russia, Poland, Hungary and Romania. Cooke (1974, p. 278) states:

> So late as 1880, there were only a quarter of a million Jews in the United States. By 1924 there were four and a half million, the product of a westward movement that started in the early nineteenth century with their exodus from the ghettos of eastern Europe into the new factories of western Europe. They had moved in that direction earlier throughout the Thirty Years War and then after the later Cossack massacres and peasant revolts. But the factory system provided them with the legal right to flee from their inferior citizenship in Germany and from pogroms in Russia, Poland and Romania. In the last quarter of the nineteenth century, both city and rural Jews were the willing quarry of emigration agents from America carrying glowing broadsides from house to house about high wages, good clothes, abundant food, and civil liberties available in the New World. The sweet talk of these promoters might be sensibly discounted, but not the bags of mail containing 'America letters' from relatives who had made the voyage and whose more practical accounts of an attainable decent life were read aloud in cottages, markets, and factories.

It is not difficult to isolate the 'push' and 'pull' factors operating in these two waves of intercontinental migration. A point worth emphasising is the significance of 'personal contact' made clear in the above passage. The feeling that the once and for all move is not into the complete unknown is very important, especially in long-distance migrations. Contemporary examples illustrating this linkage factor would include Britons migrating to Australia and West Indians migrating to Britain.

The most recent influx of people into the United States involves the Caribbean and Mexico which is, of course, contiguous with the United States of America. The peak year for European immigration was 1907 when the United States admitted 1,285,000 people. It is likely that this figure would have been surpassed in the years after the First World War had it not been for the government introducing a strict limit on immigration by means of a quota system. The quota, as it was fixed in 1927, for example, was for only

Table 3.2   Migrant workers employed in the EEC: numbers in ('000s)

Country of origin	Country of employment									
	Belgium (1972)	Denmark (1971)	W. Germany (1973)	France (1972)	Ireland (1972)	Italy (1971)	Luxembourg (1972)	Netherlands (1972)	Uk (1971)	Community total (1973)
Spain	30.0	—	179.4	270.0	—	2.0	1.2	14.8	30.0	527.0
Greece	7.0	—	268.0	5.0	—	0.7	—	1.1	50.0	332.0
Yugoslavia	1.2	14.2	466.1	50.0	—	4.1	0.5	8.8	4.0	535.0
Portugal	3.5	—	69.0	380.0	—	0.6	8.0	2.5	5.0	469.0
Turkey	12.0	—	528.2	18.0	—	0.3	—	20.8	3.0	582.0
Algeria	3.0	—	2.0	450.0	—	—	—	—	0.6	456.0
Morocco	16.5	—	15.3	120.0	—	—	—	14.2	2.0	168.0
Tunisia	2.1	10.6	11.2	60.0	—	—	—	—	0.2	74.0
Other	18.0	—	239.6	130.0	—	18.2	2.3	9.7	918.2	1,348.0
Total	93.3	24.8	1,778.8	1,483.0	0.8	25.9	12.0	71.9	1,013.0	4,491.0

(*Source:* Parker 1981)

150,000 from the whole of Europe. Migration from Mexico and Latin America, however, was unrestricted and large numbers of Puerto Ricans especially took advantage of the opportunities in the northern cities. More recently various controls on immigration have been introduced even for these neighbouring countries. However, the number of Mexicans now living and working in the United States is estimated to be several millions, the exact figure being impossible to ascertain because many are there without legal status. Indeed, this point should serve to emphasise to us the power of attraction of the 'pull factors' (mainly jobs) in a country juxtaposed to another in which a significant 'push factor' (mainly the lack of employment opportunities) exists.

Although we have concentrated here on the Americas, we should not forget that migrations for work still occur in Europe, although it is today more common for such workers to receive only temporary permits to stay in another country. The scale of these moves is outlined in table 3.2.

3.4 The changing nature of migration in Britain

The examples of Latin American immigration to the United States underlines the fact that in developing nations there lies still an 'economic imperative' behind migration. However, within the developed nations we can identify increasingly migrations that do not owe their existence primarily to such motives.

In Britain, for example, the elderly are showing far greater mobility than ever before. In 1970–71 about 60,000 people aged 60 and above migrated across a regional boundary in England and Wales, which means that approximately 5 per cent of this age group moved in that year alone.

Given the age of these migrants, it is implausible that jobs are their goal or that employment is a stimulus. Indeed, as figure 3.3 shows, the attractions are based far more upon leaving industrial and employment centres, and heading for the periphery.

1. Which areas are supplying most of the migrants, and why do people want to leave these areas?

2. What is it about the ultimate destinations that attracts the migrants?

Discussion

In your answers to the simple questions above, you may have provided equally simple observations. For example, you may have suggested that people are leaving London because it is an unpleasant environment, and they are heading for the 'Costa Geriatrica' where the weather is perceived to be warmer.

However, there are some additions we must consider.

1. The differential rates of migration between north and south must be explained. This is *not* simply a function of push factors – after all, there are many unpleasant environments in the north – but out-migration from these localities is low.

2. A major point to consider is that all moves are costly. This is especially important if neither the husband or wife is working. Research shows that as a result most retired migrants are home-owners, who can finance their move by selling their property.

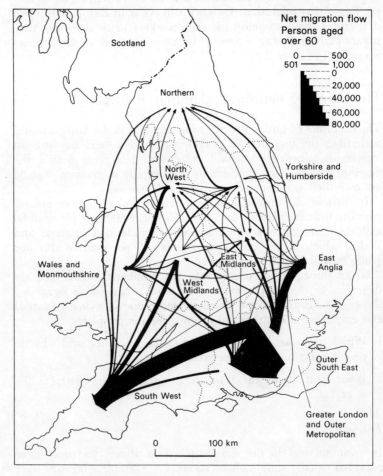

Figure 3.3   Net inter-regional migrations of those aged 60 and above, 1966–71
(Source: *Law and Warnes, 1980*)

Because house prices are so high in the southeast of England, this means that people selling their homes have far greater amounts of cash to finance the move and the purchase of a retirement home.

3. In relation to housing, figure 3.3 shows clearly that much movement is to coastal areas, where over the years specific types of housing provision have grown up, residential hotels, maisonettes and numerous bungalows, which are particularly suited to the needs of old people.

4. Furthermore, in such areas local authorities are now adept at dealing with the needs of the elderly, and there are specialised health and social services. For many widowed individuals, there is also the attraction of a supportive community – and even the chance of a new marriage.

5. Finally, let us not overlook the basic principles of interaction. Once again a distance decay function is operational. The vast majority of migrants move comparatively short distances, and very few travel far from their erstwhile friends, neighbours and, of course, their relations.

3.5 Migration and the urban fabric

Although the examples that we have already discussed involve families and individuals relocating themselves, sometimes across enormous distances, we should not neglect the small moves that are constantly occurring within our urban areas. Many of these 'migrations' barely deserve the term; many families move only a few streets, or from one neighbourhood to another. Nevertheless, the *overall* impact of these *individual* moves is large, as table 3.3 shows.

Table 3.3   Intra-urban change in Britain, 1951–71

Area*	Population		Employment	
	1951–61	*1961–71*	*1951–61*	*1961–71*
Urban cores	486,000	−729,000	902,000	−439,000
	1.9%	−2.8%	6.7%	−3.1%
Inner Metropolitan rings	1,721,000	2,512,000	293,000	707,000
	13.3%	17.2%	6.6%	15.0%
Outer rings	245,000	786,000	−14,000	130,000
	3.1%	9.8%	−0.4%	3.9%

Source: adapted from Drewett, Goddard and Spence, 1976, p. 11
* for definitions, see figure 3.4

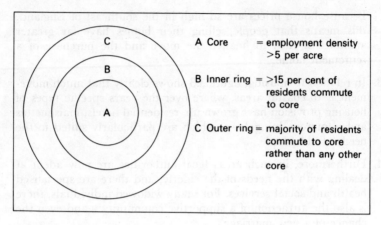

Figure 3.4   Cores, inner and outer rings, which together make up the metropolitan area

The above view of urban areas is based upon a three fold division. In the centre is the core, the employment focus, that still possesses 50 per cent of the country's jobs and approximately half its population (1971 figures). Around this are areas (the inner ring) which serve as a commuting hinterland; here are approximately one-third of the country's population, and a quarter of the jobs. Further out still is a zone (the outer ring) which represents deep suburbia; here are approximately 16 per cent of the population. A majority travel to the nearest core, although others will travel to neighbouring cores elsewhere.

Within the definitions used here, areas beyond the outer rings may be regarded as rural; these contain 4 per cent of the national population. This serves to remind us that urban, suburban and rural Britain do not constitute a fixed or static pattern. The distribution of population is still evolving, albeit as a result of thousands of individual actions. This is not to say, of course, that there have not existed similar pressures exerted upon these many individual families. The desire to move to suburban locations has been a constant feature of the housing market over the last quarter of a century, and this has been facilitated by increases in personal mobility. The removal of Victorian slums from the inner cities, and the construction of a new council housing estates on the edges of cities has also added to this trend.

Interestingly, jobs have not exerted a pull factor in these small-scale relocations. Although table 3.3 shows that employment has also diminished in the cores, it should be stressed that this has occurred rather more slowly than population movement, and has happened for very different reasons, mainly to do with urban redevelopment. In other words, the jobs have followed the people, and not vice versa.

Discussion

We have become accustomed to our cities expanding, a process that has been evident throughout the last century. As transport technology has spasmodically improved, it has become increasingly possible for residents to distance themselves from their work. The sheer scale of these changes causes us to regard them as 'normal'; we should not however lose sight of the enormity of the process. In the United States, for example, it is usual to cite the movement of blacks from the Southern states to the northern cities, like Detroit or Chicago, as one of the major contemporary migrations. Certainly, something in the region of 2,600,000 blacks moved north between 1950 and 1970. However, in the same period, 10.7 million whites also moved, leaving the cities for the new suburbs.

These suburbanites may not see themselves as migrants. Unlike the blacks, they have not moved solely out of economic necessity, they have not disrupted their lives and left family and friends behind. Nonetheless, the *overall* impact of their modest movements, in both the United States and the United Kingdom, has been enormous. We can summarise the impacts as follows:

1. *Land* In the United Kingdom, the net transfer of agricultural land to urban uses was on average virtually 20,000 ha p.a. throughout the 1960s, and only slightly less today. Much of this land is in lowland areas, and although the loss of good, productive soils has not resulted in falling agricultural output, it has certainly resulted, via higher land prices, in more expensive farming and dearer food.

2. *Cities* The barely-controlled spread of concrete across the southeast of Britain, the Eastern Seaboard of the United States, and the Ruhrgebiet of West Germany has resulted in urban areas so large that the problem of providing services such as transport can at times appear insurmountable. Furthermore, there are many observers who distinguish definite *diseconomies of scale* in the megalopolis, due to high crime rates, ill-health, congestion, homelessness and so on. These of course affect those trapped in the inner cities, in other words, those who cannot join in the exodus to the suburbs. These are issues we will examine again, in greater detail, in Books 3 and 4. This question reminds us that there exist constraints upon most forms of interaction, as we shall see below.

3.6 Constraints upon movement

We have already touched upon the far tighter controls that now limit free movement about the world. Within the last 50 years, passports have been introduced, along with immigration quotas and often even exit restrictions. As we have seen, even when workers are allowed into a developed nation, they are frequently refused citizenship and the opportunity to bring their families. They remain – sometimes for many years – temporary 'guests' (the German term 'Gastarbeiter' is an explicit recognition of this).

The net result of this weight of restrictions is that the mass migrations of the nineteenth century have ceased. Immobility – and often economic hardship – is more usual. Only rarely do sudden influxes of migrants appear, and often their migration is a spontaneous reaction of traumatic circumstances at home, and in the face of immigration controls elsewhere.

Various examples of these flights from hostile countries are shown in table 3.4, which shows the origins of nearly 4,000 refugees to this country, who were helped by the British Council for Aid to Refugees. In each case, these are individuals and families who have sought asylum in the United Kingdom rather than entering under normal immigration quotas.

The table is a depressing outline of repression within the world. The largest group has come from Vietnam, where the 'boat-people' of the South have fled in the face of invasion from North Vietnam; they dominate the table in quantitative terms, but there are other examples here of refugees leaving virtually every type of government.

1. Examine table 3.4, and pick out those groups of refugees in excess of ten persons. What do the countries of origin have in common; are they in the main repressive socialist states, fascist dictatorships, or countries troubled by civil war or invasion?

2. Table 3.4 also contains echoes of many past waves of refugees, from Hungary, for example. In order that we underline the persistence of the suffering of refugees, you should attempt to find the original reasons for their leaving their home countries (the figures in brackets refer to numbers arriving in the United Kingdom). Contemporary newspapers (available in libraries) or *Whitaker's Almanack* are both good historical sources.
   (a) Second World War refugees (2,000): 1951–56; those made stateless by the redrawing of Europe's boundaries.
   (b) Hungary (20,000): 1956.
   (c) Czechoslovakia (900): 1968.

Table 3.4   The origins of refugees arriving in the United Kingdom, 1979–80; note that the British Council for Aid to Refugees deals with approximately half those arriving in Britain

In the 12-month period between 1 October 1979 and 30 September 1980 BCAR received and assisted 3,764 new refugees. Compared with the previous year's total of 1,771 this figure, which is broken down by nationalities below, speaks for itself.

Nationality	Number of persons	Nationality	Number of persons
1 Afghanistan	33	25 Lebanese	2
2 Argentinian	1	26 Laotian	39
3 Bolivian	2	27 Liberian	4
4 Bulgarian	3	28 Libyan	9
5 Burmese	6	29 Namibian	2
6 Chilean	18	30 Nigerian	1
7 Chinese	1	31 Pakistani	9
8 Columbian	5	32 Palestinian	3
9 Cuban	2	33 Polish	12
10 Czech	24	34 Rumanian	9
11 Egyptian	1	35 Russian	3
12 El Salvadorean	2	36 Rwandan	1
13 Eritrean	45	37 Seychellois	3
14 Ethiopian	27	38 Somali	13
15 Ghanaian	32	39 South African	28
16 Greek	2	40 Sudanese	4
17 Grenadan	6	41 Syrian	3
18 Guatemalan	2	42 Tanzanian	2
19 Haitian	1	43 Ugandan	28
20 Hungarian	35	44 Vietnamese	3,223
21 Iranian	33	45 Yugoslav	2
22 Iraqi	5	46 Zairean	11
23 Kenyan	1	47 Zimbabwean	53
24 Kurdish	12	Stateless	1

Total 3,764

(*d*) Ugandan Asians (250: note many more had British passports and were thus not 'refugees'): 1973–74.
(*e*) Chileans and other Latin Americans (3,000): 1973–79.
(*f*) Indo-China (12,800): 1975–80.

Discussion

It may seem strange to use refugees as an example of constraints upon migration. However, we should not forget that their flight is a desperate response to an inability to leave by legal means. For every individual who leaves, there are no doubt many more who would dearly love to do so.

This example underlines the general conclusion that *'non-behaviour'* is often as interesting and important as behaviour. Moreover, we do not have to look to examples of repression to find numerous instances of constraints which inhibit or even entirely stop movement, migration or interaction. In daily contexts, many individuals suffer a wide range of constraints, some of which are summarised below:

1. *Time* Research is increasingly showing that many households face problems because of the difficulties of synchronising the 'time needs' of different members. For example, a single-parent may find it difficult to find work if (s)he has to travel several miles to a crêche or school before work; the problem is more difficult if work finishes later than school.

2. *Skills* As unemployment rises in the developed economies, it becomes more noticeable that it is frequently concentrated in particular regions and parts of cities. It is tempting for politicians to suggest that the unemployed should simply migrate to other areas, where the jobs are available. However, it is frequently the case that the skills possessed by a redundant steel worker from Consett or Corby are not those required in Milton Keynes. (Of course, this is even more true of those who would like to leave Turkey or Pakistan to work in Britain; the mismatch between skills and jobs is becoming larger and larger.)

3. *Housing* As we shall see in Book 4, migration within the Victorian city was a simple affair. Even the wealthy rented their homes; when they tired of them, they moved elsewhere. Now, this is not possible. Half the population owns a home but some parts of the country, notably the southeast, are very expensive. A third rents from the local authority but their chances of transferring from one local authority to another are very slight, due to housing shortages. Only those who still rent from landlords are mobile but they are frequently the ones with the lowest incomes and the least ability to move.

The question of constraint is an important one and we now summarise this point by a further quotation; commenting upon housing matters, Gray (1975, p. 230) states:

> There is an accumulating body of evidence . . . that people are not free to choose and prefer from a range of options . . . Instead, many groups are constricted and constrained from choice and pushed into particular housing situations because of their position in the housing market, and by the individuals and institutions (that is, building societies, estate agents, public and private landlords) controlling the operation . . . of housing . . .

As we shall see, housing is a key constraint upon many households' behaviour, within cities, between cities, and between regions. We must avoid falling into the trap of assuming that because people do not move, or migrate, they are completely happy with their surroundings.

3.7 Conclusions

Migrations, as we have seen in this chapter, range over enormous distances, and even within prosperous Europe, single men may leave their communities to find work.

We should end this chapter, though, by underlining the fact that the constraints upon movement are real, and are growing greater. Increasingly, some movements are leaving certain people behind, which reminds us that *'non-behaviour'* is often as interesting to study as *'behaviour'*.

In the next chapter, we shall overlook human movements entirely, in order to concentrate upon the movement of other phenomena.

Key Issues

MIGRATION Migration is a particular form of population movement, or interaction; its distinguishing feature is that it involves the relocation of the individual. In other words, the mover finds a new home in a new location and it is, therefore, the third component of population changes in a country or region after the number of births and the number of deaths:

Population change = No. of births – no. of deaths ± migration.

Migration has been studied for a considerable period of time now, partly because information on migration – in census records, for example – has been well documented. As long ago as 1887 Ravenstein was able to identify a series of 'laws' which described the general patterns of migrations. These can be found in detail in G. J. Demoko *et al.*, *Population Geography*, 1970 pp. 288–98, but it is interesting to note that several of the 'laws' concern concepts which we have used in connection with inter- action in general; law number seven stating that most migrations are short-distance ones, identifies the *distance decay effect* whereas law number five, referring to the fact that most long-distance migrants were male, is surely a comment on unequal *mobility*. With reference to section 3.2, Ravenstein clearly stated in his sixth law that most nineteenth-century population growth in urban areas in Britain was caused by in-migration.

PUSH AND PULL FACTORS Although the general *patterns* of migra- tions are quite readily described, the *process* behind the patterns is not necessarily so easy to identify. However, we can assume that:

1 The potential migrant has a good reason, or set of reasons, to force him or her to consider making such a bold decision as to move away from home permanently.
2 Once the decision to move has been taken, the chosen desti- nation must have some positive, attractive quality.

These two influences on the decision-making process are class- ified as 'push' and 'pull' factors respectively.

We have seen that this simple scheme helps us explain many migrations but we must remember that, although this kind of explanation is valid on a general level, it does not enable us to predict the actual movement and destination of the individual. Furthermore, we should not forget that very often there are serious constraints on the individual affecting the freedom of his or her choice; perhaps the most extreme examples of this are the millions of refugees in the world who have been forced to leave their homes (by hunger or for religious or political reasons) and who have no destination.

4
Diffusion

4.1 Definitions

Interaction is not simply the movement of people from place to place, or goods from location to location. Ideas also 'behave' spatially, and travel about the world. Bronowski, in his discussion of humanity's evolution, identifies the way in which concepts and beliefs spread (1973, p. 162):

> Knowledge often makes prodigious journeys and what seems to us a leap in time often turns out to be a long progression from place to place, from one city to another.

We can measure the rippling outwards of many new ideas, from the spread of Christianity from the Middle East 2,000 years ago to its modern equivalents; the DIFFUSION of fashions such as rock and roll in the 1950s, the Beatles in the 1960s, and Macdonalds in the 1970s all of which left Britain or America and spread throughout the world.

We have used here the term 'diffusion', by which we mean the spread of anything new or different from a starting point to surrounding territory. This is quite distinct from migration, which is used solely with respect to people. Usually, the term implies a friction of distance, with distant locations hearing about the innovation long after the areas closer to the source. As we shall see, this is not always the case, and of course the friction of distance itself is changing. Whereas ideas once travelled by word of mouth, and then by book or letter, they have more recently been disseminated by record, satellite and airwaves.

4.2 Models of diffusion

There are three distinct models of diffusion, *expansion*, *relocation*, and *hierarchy*.

1. *Expansion* The simplest type of process operates in the following way. In figure 4.1(a), we may note a single innovator. This

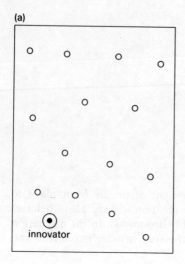

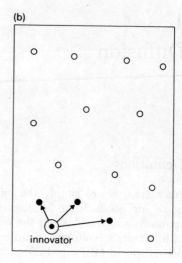

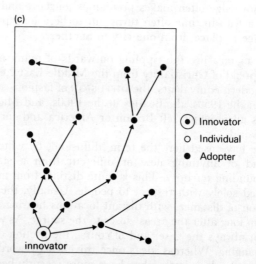

Figure 4.1   Expansion diffusion: the spread of an innovation to individuals by means of personal contact over three time periods

individual is in sole possession of an idea or a piece of information; the classic example, studied in Sweden, considered farmers adopting a new subsidy given by the government to improve their land. This farmer then tells his neighbours about the success achieved with the innovation, and they in turn adopt the subsidy. In figure 4.1(b), we can see therefore that our innovator has been joined by neighbouring adopters. Eventually, the whole community will be convinced, and the process of diffusion will be complete (figure 4.1(c)). The speed of the process will of course depend upon the friction of distance. In areas where mobility is constrained (either for physical or technological reasons), the process will be very slow. In other areas,

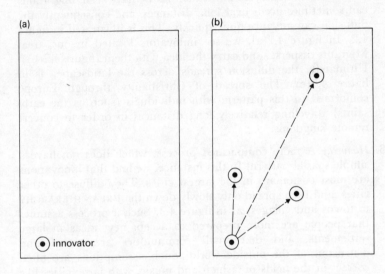

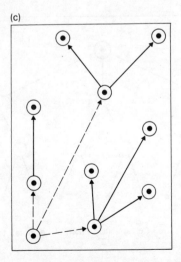

Figure 4.2 Relocation diffusion: the spread of an innovation by means of the migration of individuals from the centre of innovation

and in other contexts, the diffusion may be very quick; the spread of new household products through a suburban housing estate might be a suitable example of the latter.

2. *Relocation* A variation on the expansion theme. In this instance, the emphasis is far more upon migration, in which case the concept is carried by an individual. As we have seen, migrations can sometimes occur over long distances, and consequently the diffusion can advance quite quickly. This is illustrated in figure 4.2. In figure 4.2(a), we see innovators located in one area. Migrants disperse, and carry the idea with them (figure 4.2(b)). Ultimately, the diffusion spreads across the landscape, as in figure 4.2(c). The spread of Christianity through Europe conformed to this pattern, with individuals (such as the early saints) travelling relatively long distances in order to convert remote kingdoms.

3. *Hierarchy* A more complicated process, which does not have a simple spatial pattern. In this instance, we find that innovations are most customary in the largest cities. They diffuse to other cities, and then spread only slowly down the URBAN HIERARCHY to towns and villages, as in figure 4.3. Such a process assumes that people are more prepared to accept new ideas in large settlements, and that small communities are closed and distrustful of the outside world. Such assumptions are often correct in the fields of fashion and music, with large cities like

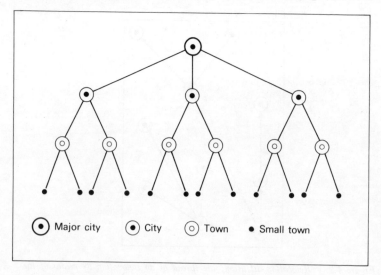

Figure 4.3   Hierarchical diffusion: the spread of an innovation through the settlement hierarchy

London and New York acting as innovators long before small settlements, which may be quite close. In other instances, there may be sound economic reasons for this process: Bradford and Kent, for example, show that commercial television stations in the United States first began in large cities, where advertising revenue was assured, and then only slowly appeared in smaller settlements (1977, p. 138). These models outline, then, three distinct processes. Let us now examine various empirical examples of them in operation.

4.3 The expansion diffusion of political ideas

Political ideas travel and spread with great rapidity. The revolutions that crossed Europe in 1848, the establishment of socialist and communist parties following the publication of *The Communist Manifesto* (also in 1848), and the creation of fascist parties in Germany, France, Italy, Spain, Britain and Norway in the years after the First World War, all indicate a diffusion process. The following example traces such a phenomenon in West Africa.

In the 1960s, political developments in Africa were extremely rapid; decolonisation and increasing wealth were responsible for a rapid rejection of many accepted ideas and patterns of government. This is not to say that change was smooth; tribal rivalries and border conflicts produced a period of intense uncertainty. What is interesting about these political developments is that they possess a geographical dimension, which is revealed in figure 4.4.

In figure 4.4(a), we can see violent political events taking place in West Africa in 1960. Coups d'état (or attempted violent changes of government) take place in Ethiopia and Congo-Kinshasa (now Zaire). In the following maps, a process of expansion diffusion can be detected, with unrest repeatedly crossing and recrossing the countries' boundaries. In 1963 (figure 4.4(b)), a coup is reported in neighbouring Congo-Brazzaville, whilst a new core of unrest is apparent in Togo and Dahomey (now Benin).

In 1964, further coups take place in Togo and Dahomey, whilst the unrest in Central Africa has spread from the Congo to Gabon (figure 4.4(c)). The following year, the same basic patterns re-emerge (figure 4.4(d)), and in 1966 a considerable expansion of violence is evident (figure 4.4(e)). Four of the states surrounding the Congo-Kinshasa undergo coups; Congo-Brazzaville, the Central African Republic, Uganda and Rwanda-Burundi. Similarly in the west, Ghana, Togo; Upper Volta and Nigeria face violent overthrow.

Let us consider how this apparent exporting of unrest and violence may proceed.

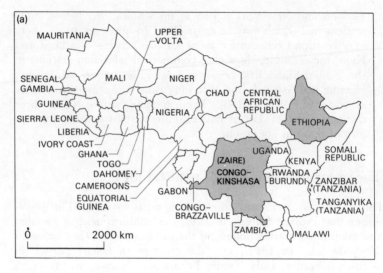

Figure 4.4   a) *Initial countries experiencing coup d'état attempts in 1960*
(Source: *Huff and Lutz, 1974*)

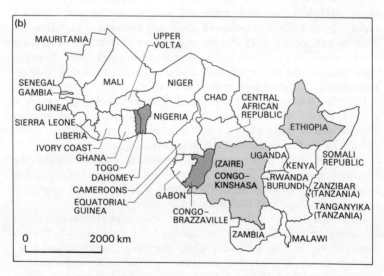

b) *Countries experiencing coup d'état attempts in 1963* (Source:
Huff and Lutz, 1974)

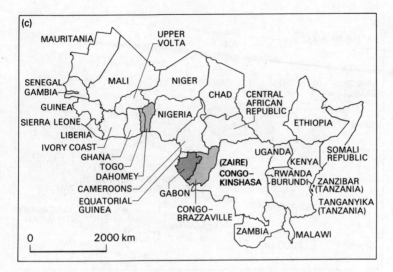

*c) Countries experiencing coup d'état attempts in 1964 (*Source: Huff and Lutz, 1974)*

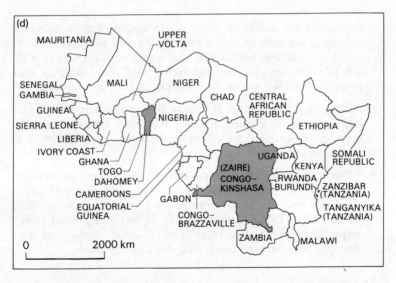

*d) Countries experiencing coup d'état attempts in 1965 (*Source: Huff and Lutz, 1974)*

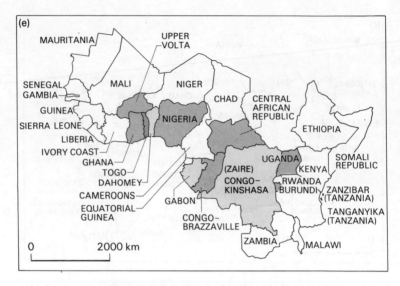

*e) Countries experiencing coup d'état attempts in 1966 (*Source:
Huff and Lutz, 1974).

1. Compile a list of factors which might account for the diffusion
   process. Take into consideration the fact that some tribal areas
   may cross national boundaries, that some countries may provide
   aid to rebels in neighbouring states, and that countries may
   preach revolution across the airwaves to their neighbours.

2. Attempt to identify other regions in the world where this process
   has occurred (*Whitaker's Almanack* is a good source of political
   events); try to map, for example, the communist takeovers in
   Southeast Asia.

3. What is meant by the 'domino theory', used to explain communist expansion, and to what extent is it a diffusion process? Is
   there any evidence that it can also work in reverse; do the events
   in Hungary (1956), Czechoslovakia (1968) and Poland (1981)
   imply that anti-Soviet ideas have diffused throughout East
   Europe, thus perhaps weakening the Eastern bloc?

Discussion

The examples taken from West Africa, Southern Africa and Southeast Asia all suggest that politics may 'spread' in a simple, spatial
way. The collapse of the existing governments in Southeast Asia –
China, North Korea, North Vietnam, South Vietnam, Cambodia –
is very reminiscent of a row of dominoes collapsing, each bringing

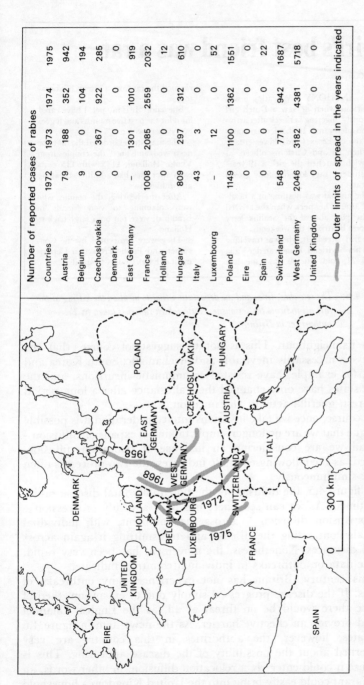

Number of reported cases of rabies					
Countries	1972	1973	1974	1975	
Austria	79	188	352	942	
Belgium	9	0	104	194	
Czechoslovakia	0	367	922	285	
Denmark	0	0	0	0	
East Germany	–	1301	1010	919	
France	1008	2085	2559	2032	
Holland	0	0	0	12	
Hungary	809	297	312	610	
Italy	43	3	0	0	
Luxembourg	–	12	0	52	
Poland	1149	1100	1362	1551	
Eire	0	0	0	0	
Spain	0	0	0	22	
Switzerland	548	771	942	1687	
West Germany	2046	3182	4381	5718	
United Kingdom	0	0	0	0	

—— Outer limits of spread in the years indicated

Figure 4.5   The spread of rabies through Western Europe during the post-war period (Source: Ministry of Agriculture, Fishery and Food)

Girl's best friend was a rat

By a Correspondent

PC ANTHONY Wheatley was suspicious when he saw a Dutch girl nervously fingering her neck after arriving on a ferry from Holland, magistrates at Harwich, Essex, were told yesterday.

When he and Customs officers at Harwich searched the girl, a 19-year-old student, they found a fully grown live rat.

The animal was nestling in a head-scarf around her neck when she arrived at the port aboard the Sealink ferry Princess Beatrix at the weekend.

Ingrid Breedvelt, who was travelling with her boyfriend, Hugo van der Valk, aged 24, told officials that she had rescued the rat from a research laboratory.

She said: "It is my pet. I have cared for it for the past five months and it goes everywhere with me."

The magistrates ordered the rat to be destroyed and fined the couple, from Venlo, Holland, £135 with £15 costs each after they had admitted breaking anti-rabies laws.

After the hearing, the couple, who were planning to visit friends in Bradford, were put on a ferry back to Holland.

They were prosecuted by the Consumer and Public Protection Department of Essex County Council.

Figure 4.6   The searches, fines and the deportation (not to mention the killing of the rat) all indicate the seriousness with which rabies is taken by the authorities in Britain

down its neighbour. This is not to suggest, of course, that the process is necessarily inevitable and mechanistic; South Korea and Laos, for example, have resisted communistic incursions, and the other states have only changed their allegiance after a long period of unrest, guerilla activity and invasion.

Of course, once we take invasions into consideration it is possible to argue that we are no longer simply talking of expansion diffusion – instead we are considering an instance of relocation diffusion. Indeed, as the following example indicates, the two processes often occur simultaneously.

In figure 4.5, the diffusion of the potentially fatal disease rabies is outlined. As we can see, there has been a steady progression – an expansion diffusion – across the continent, with individual animals contracting the disease and transmitting it again across small distances. Nonetheless, the movement has been very rapid, as the data on outbreaks in individual countries indicate.

This century, Britain has not experienced any outbreaks of rabies. If the disease progressed simply due to expansion. then of course there would be no threat at all, as the English Channel would provide an effective barrier. As the news item in figure 4.6 indicates, however, the authorities in this country are very concerned about the possibility of the disease appearing. This is because it could enter via a relocation diffusion, in other words, an immigrant could easily bring into the United Kingdom a household pet which had the disease without its having been diagnosed. No

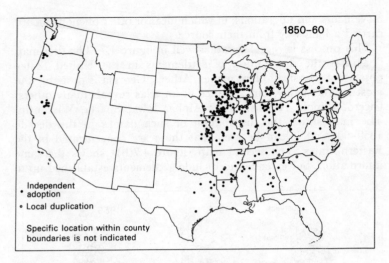

Figure 4.7   *a) Adoption of classical place names, 1850–60 (*Source: *Wilbur Zelinsky, 1967)*

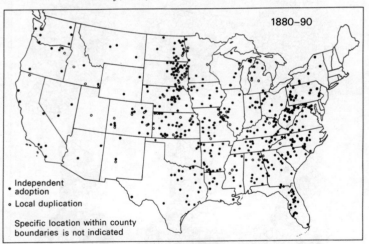

*b) Adoption of classical place names, 1880–90 (*Source: *Wilbur Zelinsky, 1967)*

doubt in other cases on the mainland too, rabies has been introduced via a long-distance relocation, and not a simple expansion process.

4.4 Relocation diffusion

Under what conditions do relocation diffusions occur? As we have already suggested, the process is associated with long-distance movements and migrations, in which ideas or other phenomena are carried a long way from their source.

This process is revealed rather well in figure 4.7. The first map illustrates the distribution of settlements in the United States possessing 'classical' place names. Athens, Georgia is probably the most famous today, but a glance at an atlas reveals many others: Cicero, Illinois; Athens, Ohio; Alpha, Iowa; Sparta, Wisconsin. The map shows the distribution of such names in the decade 1850–60, and it can be seen that these are concentrated in the Eastern states. The second map (figure 4.7(b)) shows the same information, but extended to include settlements established up to

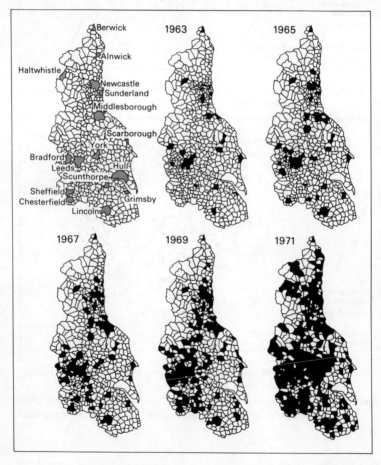

Figure 4.8   *The spread of STD telephone, by exchange areas, in northeastern England. (Comparable data not available in the Hull Corporation telephone area.) (Source: Clark, 1974)*

1890. As we can see, the pattern of place names has expanded out across the Midwest.

1. Explain why the settlement pattern in 1850–60 is confined to the area east of Kansas City. What changes in the physical environment occur at this frontier?

2. What happened between 1860 and 1880 to push the settlement pattern westwards, which allowed the migrants to establish further new settlements (some with classical names)?

4.5 Hierarchical diffusion

So far then, we have concentrated on diffusions which emanate from a source and spread across the landscape, albeit in different ways and at different speeds. In this section, we turn to the rather different process whereby a diffusion is seen to move down the urban hierarchy almost regardless of spatial factors.

Our example deals with the introduction of STD telephone exchanges in northeastern England; as the name suggests, subscriber trunk dialling (STD) is an innovation which allows greater flexibility in telephone traffic, by eliminating the need for operators to connect all long-distance calls. Figure 4.8 shows the way in which the innovation spread through northeastern England between 1963 and 1971.

1. Which locations constitute the innovators in 1963? Take a note of the places and the size of their populations.

2. Which locations become adopters in 1965? Again, take a note of their populations, and compare them with those recorded above.

3. Provide a description of the STD diffusion process between 1963 and 1971. How many processes are in evidence?

Discussion

The STD example is a good instance of a hierarchical diffusion. The initial innovators are the large centres of population such as Leeds and Lincoln, where the major telephone exchanges are located, and the system then slowly moves to smaller exchanges. Two points should be noted, however. The first is that in some parts of the region, one exchange will cater for a large rural area: Berwick is an obvious example. Consequently, Berwick is an innovator, despite its relatively small population, because it is a local 'capital' as far as telephone traffic is concerned. The second point to notice is that the diffusion is not strictly hierarchical after the initial stage; instead, STD exchanges seem to spread in the more familiar expansion form. This example suggests that in the real world, processes may be rather more complicated than we might expect, and that at times a phenomenon can diffuse by more than one of the methods that we have described.

4.6 Simulating a diffusion

The examples that we have used above show that diffusion processes in the real world are rarely as straightforward as we might hope. Consequently, it is often useful to *simulate* the process of a diffusion, in order to understand fully what has happened, is happening, or may happen in the future.

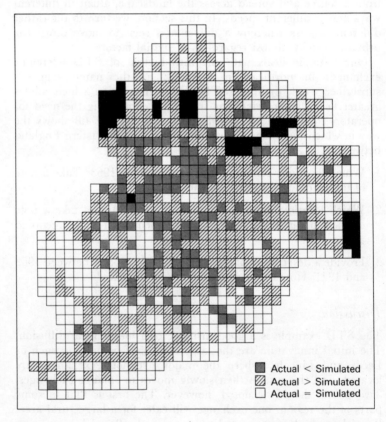

Actual < Simulated
Actual > Simulated
Actual = Simulated

Figure 4.9   a) Simulation model of immigrant population in Birmingham: 'ghetto effect'. Scale: four squares = 1 km². Note: solid black areas indicate industrial areas, large parks, etc.

There are various types of SIMULATION model. The most famous is that derived by the Swedish geographer Hägerstrand to study innovations in Asby, and it is fully described in books by Bradford and Kent (1977, pp. 128–35) and Tidswell, (1976, pp. 111–14). Basically, the simulation requires the researcher to decide upon certain rules, such as that an innovator will only pass on his or her information within a 1 km radius, due to the distance decay effect. All the individuals in an area are then identified by a number and the simulation begins. By throwing dice or using random number tables, we allow chance to dictate which neighbours are to become adopters, and which adopters will pass on the innovation again; the simulation continues until all the individuals are informed.

Simulations are useful because they help us to spot factors which aid or inhibit diffusion. For example, a simulation might predict

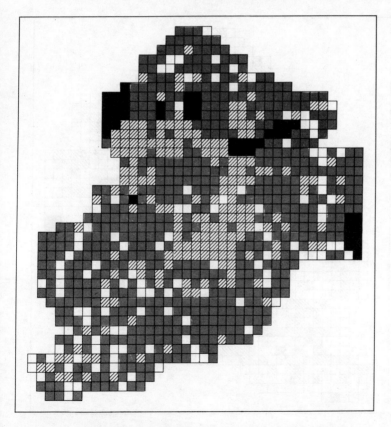

b) Simulation model of immigrant population in Birmingham: 'suburban effect'. Note: solid black areas indicate industrial areas, large parks, etc.

that all potential adopters accepted the innovation within a short time period, whereas in reality some did not. Clearly, we would have to change the rules, and slow the model down – perhaps by shortening the distance–decay field, so that innovators only pass information across 0.5 km. When the simulation is successful, it can therefore help us to pinpoint what is happening in reality, without having to mount expensive surveys.

Many of the simulation exercises undertaken have concentrated upon the spread of innovations, although it is just as easy to use the technique to study the movement of people. An example of this is shown in figure 4.9, which shows three attempts to simulate the movements of black families in Birmingham between 1961–71. The city has been divided up into small zones, and a simulation of the population change for all the zones attempted. Figure 4.9(a)

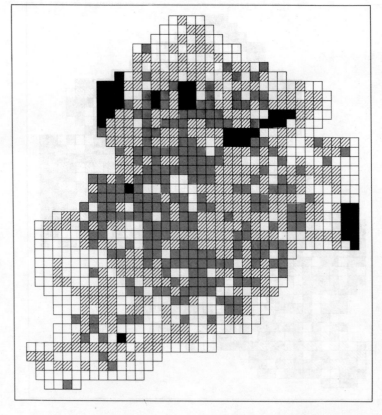

c) Simulation model of immigrant population in Birmingham:
'housing effect'. Note solid black areas indicate industrial areas,
large parks, etc. (Source: *Woods, 1975*).

assumed that immigrants arriving in the city would settle in direct proportion to the existing pattern of black families; as the diagram shows however, this simulation produced far too much of a concentration – a GHETTO EFFECT – in the centre of Birmingham.

Figure 4.9(b) consequently changes the 'rules' slightly. In this instance, 5 per cent of the immigrants are annually allowed to spread away from the original concentrations of black families. However, in this case, the simulation produces too many black households in the suburbs; in other words, the simulation has been too optimistic about the immigrants' mobility.

The third map (figure 4.9(c)) is the most successful. In this case, the simulation model has assumed that blacks can only move to population zones if there exists there a type of housing known as *multiple-occupancy*, houses which people can share, thus reducing the costs of accommodation.

Discussion

These three simulation models show that black families are mobile within Birmingham (and probably other British cities), but not completely so – they do not tend to move out to suburban areas a great deal. This is because they tend to prefer multiply-occupied housing, because of its cheapness and convenience, and such housing is not found in some parts of the city, such as the suburbs. We might have anticipated this finding, but the simulation model confirms our suspicions quickly and easily.

Key Issues

DIFFUSION Diffusion is the general heading given to any process which enables an innovation to be slowly taken up, or adopted, by more and more people in an area. 'Innovations' can be thought of as phenomena such as fashions of clothing or music, information on government or EEC grants available to small firms or farms, or even a disease. In each case there is an 'innovator' (someone who introduces the innovation for the first time) and increasing numbers of 'adopters' (people who catch the disease, take up the new fashion and so on). We have identified three types of diffusion, expansion, relocation and hierarchical diffusion, but we should remember that these processes are not mutually exclusive; it is possible that all three types might operate at the same time on the same innovation, but, of course, in different ways.

URBAN HIERARCHY Hierarchical diffusion is seen to operate through the urban hierarchy. In general, the settlements of a country or region are arranged in a hierarchy; in other words we can list the settlements in order of size and importance (the latter meaning the number of shops and other service functions the settlement possesses). When this is done, we normally find that there are very few large, important settlements and large numbers of small, far less important settlements. Indeed in many countries there is just one dominant city at the top of the hierarchy which is important enough to be considered a 'world city'; London, Paris, New York, Rio de Janeiro and Tokyo are some examples.

If we take the adoption of new Paris fashions by the British as an example, it is clear that people living in London are likely to be the first adopters, followed by people in the next layer of the hierarchy (Birmingham, Manchester, Leeds) and so on. A full discussion on the urban hierarchy can be found in Bradford and Kent (1977, ch. 1 pp. 22–24).

SIMULATION A simulation is rather like an experiment. If the experiment is successful it means that we can recreate a general diffusion pattern according to our pre-decided rules. The very fact that we know the 'rules of the game' often helps us understand the real-life diffusion better, or even predict how fast or slow and in which directions the diffusion of an innovation is going to occur in the future. A crucial point here is that simulations usually incorporate a random or chance element and for this reason dice or 'random number tables' are required. This is not an unrealistic feature of simulations. In fact, far from it, as the Paris fashions example shows; we can only say that Londoners are *more likely* to adopt the innovation first. It is not *impossible* for the first adopter to be a rural dweller, although it is *unlikely*.

GHETTO EFFECT When a part of a city is almost exclusively occupied by one group of people, usually immigrants, it is described as a ghetto. The ghetto can often be identified by the observer not only by the concentration of people of a certain type living there but by the lack of services and the physical deterioration of the buildings. The reasons why ghettos form in particular areas of the city and not others are complex. However, it is unlikely that ghettos would grow into the suburbs (which are isolated from places of work and where high rates of car-ownership are necessary) and it is more likely that they will grow in areas where dwellings suitable for *multiple occupancy* are available (larger buildings such as tenements or Victorian 'villas' in which several family units can live). Both these factors relate to the fact that immigrants are frequently low-wage earners, and thus very constrained in terms of their residential choices within the city.

5
Conclusion

5.1 Regions and interaction

In the first book in the *Space and Society* series, we examined regions, or the ways in which groups and individuals divide up the environment – into administrative areas, or perceptual areas – and the ways in which the landscape itself possesses natural divisions. In this book, we have considered *interaction*, and the ways in which groups and individuals move through space, in order to communicate and act with each other and to use phenomena such as shops or entertainments. Together, the two books account for the most basic concerns of the geographer.

Twenty years ago, geographers expected that they would eventually be able to produce laws to account for all types of movement and interaction. The predictability of aggregate activity – as opposed to individual behaviour, which always varies slightly from person to person – suggested that it would eventually be possible to reduce all interaction to a few simple equations. Some geographers (and planners) have sought these elusive equations; they view cities as follows:

1. Imagine a certain quantity of industrial activity (e), employing a particular number of employees (E), at location (j); the number of employees is proportional to, or a function of (f), the amount of activity;

$$E = f(e).$$

2. Find homes for these employees (E), remembering that the friction of distance dictates that the majority will want to live close to their work – in residential neighbourhood (i);

$$Ri = f(cij)$$

The number of residents in an area (Ri) is thus larger if the costs (c) of travelling to work (at j) from homes (in i) are low, and smaller if the distance is large and the costs high.

3. Build services like shops (S) for these residents, bearing in mind that

$$Si = f(Ri)$$

that is, that a number of residents can only support a certain number of shops.

Also bear in mind that the shops must not be too far away; in location k;

$$Sk = f(cik).$$

In other words, another distance–decay effect is in operation.

4. The model carries on, using the same logic – the shopworkers need homes, and we assign these again using a distance decay approach. More homes mean shops, and so on.

5.2 Other applications

This view of the world works, and is useful if we are planning something like a new town 'from scratch'. Unfortunately, the geographers' dream of creating a predictable world has faded; the falling birth rate means we are no longer building new towns, and instead we are trying to improve the quality of life in the towns and cities that we already possess. This means that planners are no longer dealing with the large schemes – new settlements, new airports – exactly those contexts in which computer models of this type are so successful.

Interestingly, the basic ideas of interaction are still useful in the new task of improving existing environments. We have seen here that the quality of life is strongly influenced by the conditions surrounding the individual, and that the environment is a constrained one: interaction is simply limited to a fairly small territory. As a result, the immediate surroundings must be stimulating, desirable and pleasant, because we spend so much time using them. To pick up our previous example once more, some new towns have been unpopular precisely because the surroundings – the action space – are so desolate, sterile and unadventurous.

Clearly, it is dangerous to overemphasise this issue. Income is still probably more important than the quality of life to many people. In both cases however, the individual response to a shortage of employment and/or a poor environment has always historically been the same – to move to a different location. Interestingly, the same 'rules' apply. Most people move the minimum distance necessary to improve their circumstances. At certain times, the conditions prevailing in certain parts of the world, and the attactions elsewhere, have dictated long migrations, sometimes from one continent to another. This is increasingly impossible, and the bulk of migrants once more move relatively short distances, perhaps from one country to another, but more usually from one region to another, or from one part of the city to another. Some, of course, cannot or will not move, and for them the quality of life may not be as high as it should be.

5.3 And other perspectives

The consideration of diffusion is really little more than the corollary of what we have already examined. In cases where people do not move to seek out new phenomena, those phenomena will frequently spread themselves through the population in due course. The introduction of cinemas may be taken here as an example. The establishment of cinemas in large cities may have been for a short while another reason for leaving small towns and villages and heading for the 'bright lights' – in this case, quite literally. In a fairly short time however, the lowliest village hall possessed its own 'kinema', and when that attraction was lost the diffusion process was complete. The specific form of diffusion varies, as we have seen, but generally the basic principles of interaction hold good. Even long-distance diffusions (such as, for example, forms of influenza which cross the world) proceed by stealth, from neighbour to neighbour, and from passenger to passenger.

Let us at this point re-emphasise one point. We can never predict the behaviour of *one* influenza germ, *one* worker travelling to a factory, *one* migrant heading for a retirement home in Hastings. All our equations are expressed in aggregate terms, so that we can predict with some confidence that in one town, X per cent of people will travel Y miles to work, or that an innovation will reach a certain destination within a certain number of years.

In summary then, we are suggesting here that spatial behaviour is often predictable, and that an understanding of phenomena such as action spaces (and the externalities within them) can go a long way towards providing an understanding of an individual's quality of life. It may sound a little lame to suggest that geography has only one law, to compete with the dozens learnt by chemists and physicists, and even lamer if that law is expressed as 'all things interact more with things close to, rather than things further away'. As we have seen, however, a great deal of human behaviour can be seen ultimately to relate to this fundamental insight.

Photographic section

1 Home improvements as externalities

The photograph shows a home extension which has encroached right up to the edge of the property, blocking light and the view from the adjoining houses; the shot is taken from a window in one of the latter. Development control – the right of the local authority to stop building developments it does not approve of – normally stops such 'improvements'. In this instance, the aggrieved owners were granted a reduction of their rateable value by the Inland Revenue, on the grounds that the intrinsic value of the properties had been lowered.

1. In how many ways could the finished extension constitute a 'nuisance'? What value could be placed upon these nuisances?

2. Can you imagine any contexts in which an extension could constitute a positive externality?

2 What price progress?

1. We have no way of knowing how primitive societies reacted to developments like fire. We do know, however, of examples of recent innovations – ones that we now regard with affection – that were originally viewed with trepidation. What examples illustrate this?

2. Is it likely that nuclear power will also enter the category of an innovation that we learn to accept and ultimately ignore, or will people always perceive there to be a negative externality field around the reactors?

3 In search of bus conductors, Trinidad

This press cutting from the *Trinidad Guardian* of 1966 reminds us that while immigration (usually 'coloured immigration') has its political opponents, there are usually real economic reasons which have encouraged the host countries to permit entry. Throughout Western Europe and America there have been cyclical labour shortages which have been met by enticing mobile foreigners. Although Algerians in France, Turks in Germany and Puerto Ricans in the USA face periodic bouts of hostility, it should be remembered that their presence has frequently followed invitation and does not constitute an uncontrolled invasion.

4 Boat people arriving in Hong Kong

This scene shows refugees from the fighting in Vietnam arriving in Hong Kong. These enforced migrants left Vietnam as a result of political and ethnic persecution following the fall of South Vietnam in 1975. Large numbers have arrived in Hong Kong in frail craft – large numbers have also died at sea. In the main, their presence is welcome in Hong Kong, whose economic miracle is based almost entirely upon very cheap and skilled labour.

1. This example underlines the fact that migrations often depend almost entirely upon push factors. List other examples that have occurred in recent years around the world.

2. Note that migrants – and refugees – depend upon other countries finding the immigrants economically or politically desirable; the USA has always welcomed Cuban emigrés, whereas Hong Kong always returns those escaping from the People's Republic of China. Suggest other examples of successful and unsuccessful mobility.

5 No pets, no rabies

This poster is to be found displayed in all airports and ports throughout the UK. Issued by the Ministry of Agriculture, Fisheries and Food in 1980, it makes the explicit point that the UK islands stand isolated from the surrounding threat of rabies.

1. The existence of the sea barrier means that Britain is in a fortunate position with regard to disease transmission. What other animal disease is endemic in Europe, but found less often here?

2. In the past, it has been relatively easy to keep out other things, foreign imports, foreign ideas, even 'undesirables' from other countries. However relatively recent changes mean that this is no longer the case. Legislation dating from 1973 means that

Britain cannot restrict imports, and new technological developments promise a flood of European TV programmes. What were these two developments?

6 Innovations: your local CB shop

This photograph, taken in 1982, shows a shop specialising in the then newly-arrived citizen band (CB) radio equipment. The very sudden arrival of CB from the USA (coupled with the excitement of its illegality) permitted a large number of shops, specialist magazines and distribution organisations to emerge. The diffusion of CB has been equally rapid, so rapid in fact that the target population of potential users has very quickly been saturated. In consequence, the specialist shops are already beginning to disappear.

1. Although this shop emphasises CB equipment, we can also see evidence of three other innovations which are now commonplace. Examine the photograph closely; note that one of the former innovations is not electronic in any way.

2. Once the initial wave of diffusion of an innovation such as CB or video is complete, the diffusion continues though in a more subdued fashion. As this evolution takes place, what kind of retailers increasingly take the role of distributors of the innovation?

Photograph 1   Home improvements as externalities

Photograph 2   What price progress?

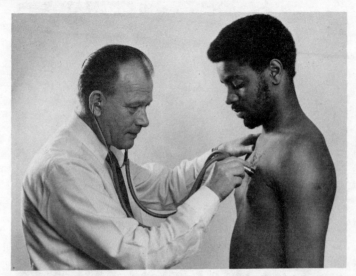

In search of bus conductors

by Ewart Rouse

SCORES of young men were interviewed yesterday at the Employment Exchange, Laventille, for possible selection as bus conductors for the London Transport Board.

At the end of the interviewing session, Mr. Charles Gomm, recruiting officer, said he had found many of them suitable for employment.

The would-be busmen were subjected to on-the-spot medical check-ups by Dr. C. N. Myers, another representative of the Board, and to intelligence tests. —**(In picture above, a confident Mr. Junior Pierre receives his check-up).**

Mr. Gomm emphasised, however, that the question of appointment would depend on how soon the men were able to get permits to work in England.

He also said that the number of conductors to be recruited would depend on how many permits the Board could obtain.

30 WORKERS A MONTH

"We are, however, aiming at the provisional figure of 30 workers a month. This is over an indefinite period," Mr. Gomm added.

Those who were found suitable were told so at the end of their interviews and check-ups.

Mr. Gomm explained that they would have to be medically examined, again shortly before departure for London.

"The final nod of approval will be given on the basis of this examination," he said.

More prospective busmen will be interviewed today and tomorrow by Mr. Gomm, who is expected to return to London shortly.

Meanwhile, domestics for recruitment for work in the United States come up for their interviews tomorrow.

It is understood that more than 700 women have submitted applications, and these are now on file at the Exchange.

The applicants are expected to turn up tomorrow with character references, among other documents.

Photograph 3   In search of bus conductors, Trinidad

Photograph 4   Boat people arriving in Hong Kong

Photograph 5   No pets, no rabies

Photograph 6   Innovations: your local CB shop

References

Bale, J., (1980), 'Football clubs as neighbours', *Town and Country Planning*, Mar. 93–94.

Bradford, M. G. and Kent, A. (1977), *Human Geography*, Oxford University Press, Oxford.

Bronowski, J. (1973), *The Ascent of Man*, BBC Publications, London.

Chapman, K. (1979) *People Pattern and Process*, Edward Arnold, London.

Clark, D. (1974), 'Technology, diffusion and time-space convergence: the example of STD telephones' *Area*, 6(3), 181–84.

Cooke, A. (1974), *America*, BBC Publications, London.

Demko, G. J, Rose, H. M. and Schnell, G. A. (1970), *Population Geography: a reader*, McGraw-Hill, New York.

Drewett, R., Goddard, J. B. and Spence, N. (1976) 'What's happening in British cities?', *Town and Country Planning*, 44(1), 14–24.

Foot, D. H. S. (1981), *Operational Urban Models: an introduction*, Methuen, London.

Gray, F. (1975) 'Non-explanation in urban geography', *Area*, 7(4), 228–34.

Haggett, P. (1979) *Geography – a modern synthesis*, McGraw-Hill, New York.

Haynes, R. M. (1974), 'Application of exponential distance decay to human and animal activities', *Geografiska Annaler*, 56B(2), 90–104.

Huff, D. L. and Lutz, J. M. (1974) 'The contagion of political unrest in independent Black Africa', *Economic Geography*, 50(4), 352–67.

Johnston, R. J. (1979) *Political, Electoral and Spatial Systems*, Oxford University Press, Oxford.

Law, C. M. and Warnes, A. M. (1980), 'The characteristics of retired migrants', in Herbert D. T. and Johnston R. J. (eds) *Geography and the Urban Environment*, John Wiley, Chichester, 175–222.

Löytönen, L. and Löytönen, M. (1980), 'Kaatopaikan haittojen levinneisyys ympäristön asukkaiden kokemana', *Terra*, 92(1), 21–27.

McBride, P. (1976), 'Hypothesis testing in sixth-form geography', *Teaching Geography*, **2**(1), 24–29.

Newby, H. (1980), *Where the Grass is Greener*, Penguin, Harmondsworth.

Parker, G. (1981), *The Logic of Unity*, Longman, London.

Smith, C. J. (1980), 'Neighbourhood effects on mental health', in Herbert, D. T. and Johnston, R. J. (eds) *Geography and the Urban Environment*, John Wiley, Chichester, pp. 363–416.

Smith, D. M. (1977), *Human Geography – a welfare approach*, Edward Arnold, London.

Tidswell, V. (1976), *Pattern and Process in Human Geography*, University Tutorial Press, London.

Tobler, W. and Wineburg, S. (1971), 'A Cappadocian experiment', *Nature*, 231, 7 May, 39–41.

Wheeler, J. O. (1976), 'Locational dimensions of urban highway impact', *Geografiska Annaler*, **58B**(2), 67–78.

Woods, R. I. (1975), 'A stochastic analysis of immigrant distributions', *Research Paper II*, Department of Geography, University of Oxford.

Zelinsky, W. (1967), 'Classical town names in the United States', *Geographical Review*, **57**, 463–95.

Zipf, G. K. (1949), *Human Behaviour and the Principle of Least Effort*, Addison-Wesley, Reading, Massachussetts, USA.